LAW FOR THE CLERGY:

A COMPILATION OF THE STATUTES

OF THE STATES OF

ILLINOIS, INDIANA, IOWA, MICHIGAN, MINNESOTA, OHIO AND WISCONSIN,

RELATING TO

THE DUTIES OF CLERGYMEN

IN THE SOLEMNIZATION OF MARRIAGE,

THE ORGANIZATION OF CHURCHES AND RELIGIOUS SOCIETIES, AND THE PROTECTION OF RELIGIOUS MEETINGS AND ASSEMBLIES,

WITH NOTES AND PRACTICAL FORMS,

EMBRACING A COLLATION OF

THE COMMON LAW OF MARRIAGE.

By SANFORD A. HUDSON,
COUNSELOR-AT-LAW.

CHICAGO:
S. C. GRIGGS AND COMPANY.
1877.

KNIGHT & LEONARD, PRINTERS, CHICAGO.

PREFACE.

THE professional duties of clergymen in the solemnization of marriage, the organization and incorporation of churches, religious societies and benevolent institutions, so often involving legal questions of importance; and realizing the necessity of a strict compliance with law in the performance of those duties, I have long been impressed with the belief that a compilation of the statutes of the several states on those subjects, with notes and practical forms, would supply a want long existing, and serve a benign purpose in the interest of that class of professional men, and the general public as well.

Clergymen, who perform the greater number of marriages, are very liable to commit errors in consequence of not having access to the statutes of the state, and those removing from one state to another will be quite likely to be deceived, as the laws of the several states on this subject differ so widely that a marriage performed according to the laws of one state would not be in conformity to those of another; and they are not always aware that a neglect of duty in some important particular may subject them to a statutory penalty. It has ever been the policy of legislatures to regulate this subject by stringent laws, which apply more particularly to the officiating minister than to the parties. They have also provided for the incorporation of churches, religious societies and institutions; and in the new states, organizations under these laws are constantly springing up, and must require an examination of them by clergymen and others, and certificates and other papers drawn *properly*, in order that such churches and societies may be so organized as to have a legal corporate existence, which without any guide, such as this work is designed to be, would require the services of a lawyer.

The statutes of the several states mentioned in the title-page relating to these subjects and to religious assemblies, and the duties of clergymen involved therein or affected thereby, have been carefully compiled, and notes and practical forms appended to the sections to which they relate for greater convenience, affording, as it is hoped, a complete guide in all those matters. In the chapter upon the Common Law of Marriage, which gives a general view of the subject, treating of the qualifications of persons to enter that state and the impediments thereto, I have quoted largely from Kent's Commentaries, Tyler's Infancy and Coverture, Bishop's Marriage and Divorce, Bingham's Law of Infancy and Coverture, as well as from the opinions and decisions of the courts in many important cases; and as the work is not intended for the legal profession, and the extracts made as above necessarily fragmentary, I do not give references.

With these prefatory remarks the work is submitted to the public, and if it shall receive the approbation of those for whom it is intended, I shall be gratified.

S. A. H.

FEBRUARY 5, 1877.

CONTENTS.

CHAPTER I.

THE COMMON LAW OF MARRIAGE, ... 7

CHAPTER II.

ILLINOIS STATUTES OF MARRIAGE, ... 29

CHAPTER III.

ILLINOIS STATUTES OF RELIGION AND RELIGIOUS ASSEMBLIES, ... 34

CHAPTER IV.

ILLINOIS STATUTES OF RELIGIOUS SOCIETIES, . 37

CHAPTER V.

INDIANA STATUTES OF MARRIAGE, ... 42

CHAPTER VI.

INDIANA STATUTES OF RELIGIOUS SOCIETIES, . 46

CHAPTER VII.

INDIANA STATUTES OF RELIGIOUS ASSEMBLIES, . 58

CHAPTER VIII.

IOWA STATUTES OF MARRIAGE, ... 62

CHAPTER IX.

IOWA STATUTES OF INCORPORATION OF RELIGIOUS SOCIETIES, ... 66

CHAPTER X.

Iowa Statutes of Religious Assemblies, . 72

CHAPTER XI.

Michigan Statutes of Marriage, . . . 75

CHAPTER XII.

Michigan Statutes of Religious Societies, . 83

CHAPTER XIII.

Michigan Statutes of Religious Assemblies, . 96

CHAPTER XIV.

Minnesota Statutes of Marriage, . . 99

CHAPTER XV.

Minnesota Statutes of Religious Assemblies, 107

CHAPTER XVI.

Minnesota Statutes of Religious Corporations, 110

CHAPTER XVII.

Ohio Statutes of Marriage, . . . 126

CHAPTER XVIII.

Ohio Statutes of Religious Assemblies, . 132

CHAPTER XIX.

Ohio Statutes of Religious Societies, . . 137

CHAPTER XX.

Wisconsin Statutes of Marriage, . . 155

CHAPTER XXI.

Wisconsin Statutes of Religious Assemblies, 163

CHAPTER XXII.

Wisconsin Statutes of Religious Societies, . 167

CHAPTER I.

THE COMMON LAW OF MARRIAGE.

Section 1. "The primary and most important of the domestic relations," says Chancellor Kent, "is that of husband and wife. It has its foundation in nature, and is the only lawful relation by which Providence has permitted the continuance of the human race. In every age it has had a propitious influence in the moral improvement and happiness of mankind; it is one of the chief foundations of social order. We may justly place to the credit of the institution of marriage a great share of the blessings which flow from refinement of manners, the education of children, the sense of justice, and the cultivation of the liberal arts."

Sec. 2. In Protestant communities marriage is not regarded as a sacrament, nor as peculiar to the church of Christ; but it is considered in all countries as the most sacred of all contracts, and in England it is celebrated as a religious ceremony. In the United States it is only a civil contract, and certain magistrates, equally with the ministers of the gospel, have the right to solemnize it, but the prevailing practice among the cultivated and refined is to have it performed by a clergyman, and attended with religious ceremonies.

Sec. 3. And while it is undoubtedly a contract, it is a contract sanctioned by law, controlled by considerations of public policy, vital to the order and harmony of social life, and in its nature indissoluble, except by violations of duty on the one part to be taken advantage of in a special manner provided by law on the other.

Sec. 4. So a judge who delivered the opinion of the court in a case in Tennessee observed: "By the English canon and ecclesiastical law, this union of marriage is of a nature so widely differing from ordinary contracts; creating disabilities and conferring privileges between husband and wife; producing interests, attachments and feelings, partly from necessity, but mainly from a principle in our nature, which together form the strongest ligament in human society, without which perhaps it could not exist in a civilized state; it is a connection of such a deep toned and solemn character, that society has even more interest in preserving it than the parties themselves."

Sec. 5. So, also, in a case in the State of Delaware, the court remarked: "The marriage contract is one of a peculiar character, and subject to peculiar principles. It may be entered into by persons who are capable of forming any other lawful contract; it can be violated and annulled by law, which no other contract can. It cannot be dissolved and determined by the will of the parties as any other contract may be, and its rights and obligations are derived rather from the law relating to it than from the contract itself."

Sec. 6. In strictness, though formed by contract it

signifies a relation or status deriving both its rights and duties from a source higher than any contract which the parties are capable of making.

Sec. 7. What is necessary to constitute a complete and valid marriage is a question which for a long time has remained in a state of singular uncertainty, if it can be regarded as definitely settled at the present day. The question whether the ceremonies and forms, or any of them, which are indicated by law, or are customarily used for the solemnization of a marriage, are indispensable to the validity of the marriage or not, has received much discussion in the courts, both in England and America, and the decisions have been far from unanimous on the subject. Sometimes it has been held that the marriage is not full and complete without both the civil and the religious ceremony, and at others that the mere consent of the parties is sufficient. It is generally understood that by the ancient common law of England, marriage being regarded as a sacrament, must, to be valid, have been celebrated *facie ecclesiæ*, but since the Reformation it has been regarded as a civil contract.

Sec. 8. That marriage might be validly contracted by mutual promises alone, or what were called "*sponsalia de præsenti*," without the presence or benediction of a priest, was an established principle of civil and common law antecedent to the Council of Trent. Previous to the marriage act, so called, of 26 George II, the legal validity of marriages depended upon the doctrines of the ecclesiastical courts. Some former statutes had inflicted penalties upon parties concerned in the celebration of clandestine marriages, but without venturing to control the rules which the church had established with reference to their validity. An opinion was commonly entertained that matrimony, ordained and regulated by the divine law, was not to be treated as a human institution, and was not a proper subject for the interference of the civil legislature.

Sec. 9. But to come down to our own time. Chancellor Kent has said: "No peculiar ceremonies are requisite by the common law to the valid celebration of the marriage; the consent of the parties is all that is regarded, and, as marriage is said to be a contract *jure gentium*, consent is all that is regarded by natural or public law. The Roman lawyers strongly inculcated the doctrine that the very foundation and essence of the contract consisted in consent, freely given by parties competent to contract. This is the language equally of the common and canon law and of common reason."

Sec. 10. And Chancellor Walworth, while he admitted that by the ancient common law of England a marriage was invalid unless it was celebrated *infacie ecclesiæ*, thought that the law on the subject was unquestionably changed at the Reformation, if not before, and unqualifiedly asserted that it is now a settled rule of the common law, which was brought into this country by its first English settlers, and which was probably the same among the ancient Protestant Dutch inhabitants, that any mutual agreement between the parties to be husband and wife *in presenti*, especially when it is followed by cohabitation, constitutes a valid and binding marriage if there is no legal disability on the part of either to contract matrimony.

Sec. 11. What constitutes marriage in itself is altogether different from the mere proof and evidence of marriage. It may be inferred from various circumstances, without weakening the argument in favor of needful legal forms in the face of some church or before some judicial tribunal.

Sec. 12. In the United States the religious form of marriage is the general rule, being imperative in some of the states, and no state or territory in the United States is without some form of marriage legislation, either statutory or under established usage.

Sec. 13. The churches and religious societies into which the Christian world had been subdivided at the period of the settlement, had full rights according to their respective creeds, and nothing better attests to the reverence for this sacred obligation under the marriage contract than the unequivocal sentiment of disgust pervading all sorts of people everywhere at the attempted introduction of polygamy into Utah, a remote wilderness, to which the Mormons had been forced solely on account of this obnoxious doctrine in defiance of morals and against common law.

Sec. 14. In England and in every state of the United States the greatest indulgence has been conceded to the Friends, called Quakers. Their mode maintains in its integrity the order of marriage and secures its due authentication; clandestineness is altogether excluded. The marriage must be in the face of a congregation duly assembled, and the mutual promise of the man and woman is attested by those present,—a practice worthy of more general imitation.

Sec. 15. Marriage in the Roman Catholic church, since the twenty-fourth session of the Council of Trent, has been regarded as a sacrament; and the Friends, called Quakers, as if in emulation, while denying the efficacy of all forms, have been at special pains to hedge the marriage ceremony in the strictest manner. Their example has not been without its salutary effect in this behalf with other denominations of Christians, with whom marriage is not a civil contract, disjoined at the option of parties from all religious forms.

Sec. 16. In general, all persons are able to contract themselves in marriage unless they labor under some particular disabilities and incapacities, there being several disabilities and incapacities, or, in other words, impediments, which disqualify the parties from entering into a valid contract of marriage. These will be noted in their order.

Sec. 17. First—Want of the requisite age to consent to the marriage, which at common law is fixed at fourteen in males and twelve in females. The law supposes that the parties below those ages have not sufficient understanding to consent to the marriage contract, and such a marriage contract may be avoided by either party to it on arriving at the age of consent. But above the ages indicated the parties are supposed to have sufficient discretion for such a contract, and they can bind themselves irrevocably.

Sec. 18. The ages at which parties may contract marriages are fixed by statute in most of the states, and in some it is required that before any marriage shall be solemnized between persons under certain ages, the consent of parents or guardians shall be produced to the officiating clergyman.

Sec. 19. All persons who have not the regular use of the understanding sufficient to deal with discretion in the common affairs of life, as idiots and lunatics (except in their lucid intervals), are incapable of agreeing to any contract, and of course to that of marriage, and marriage with an idiot or lunatic is absolutely void; and a marriage would be void if made while one of the parties was in a state of intoxication, such as would incapacitate the party from entering into any other contract.

Sec. 20. Second—A marriage procured by force or fraud is also void *ab initio*, and may be treated as null by every court in which its validity may be called in question, as fraud vitiates all contracts. The basis of the marriage contract is consent, and the ingredient of fraud or duress is as fatal in this as in any other contract, for the free assent of the mind is wanting.

Sec. 21. It is not, however, every misrepresentation or deception that will affect the validity of the marriage. The law presumes that a person uses due caution in a matter in which his happiness for life is so materially involved as in that of matrimony, and it therefore makes no provision for the relief of a blind credulity, howsoever it may have been produced. All those deceptive acts to which the sexes too frequently have recourse with a view to obtain what they consider an advantageous connection, by setting off their persons, characters, tempers, circumstances and connection in a too favorable light; or by professions of ardent affection which they either may not feel, or not in a degree equal to what they profess; though they meet with various degrees of indulgence according to circumstances, are still inconsistent with truth and sincerity, and may be, and often are, productive of serious mischief. They partake of the nature of fraud, but hardly amount to enough to avoid a contract of marriage.

Sec. 22. But the authorities are clear that when there is actual fraud in the transaction, a marriage, like all other contracts, may be avoided by the party injured. In a late case in New York, the Chancellor found that the marriage in the case was procured by fraud, saying that the woman had been entrapped into the marriage with the man by the artifices which he employed, and although she gave an apparent consent at the moment of celebration, yet it fully appeared that this consent was feigned, and that it was the effect, not of her choice, but of her terror. The complainant had never consented freely to become the wife of the defendant and had never cohabited with him, and the marriage was declared to be a foul fraud upon her by the defendant, and on that ground was adjudged to be utterly null and dissolved.

Sec. 23. And here it may be well to distinguish between contracts which are void and those which are voidable. The first are as though nothing had been done, absolutely without any force or life. The latter are binding, unless one of the parties sees fit to repudiate it; being under the age of consent, either may annul it on arriving at the age of consent, but if they continue to cohabit on arriving at that age the contract is binding ever after.

Sec. 24. With respect to the difference between void and voidable marriages, a very able and learned judge of North Carolina has said: "There is a distinction in the law between void and voidable marriages wherever they were regularly solemnized. The latter, which are sometimes called marriages *de facto*, are such as are contracted between persons who have capacity to contract, but are forbidden by law from contracting with each other; but until the nullity is declared as an existing marriage, it was recognized as valid both in the canon and common law. But when the marriage is between persons, one of whom has no capacity to contract at all, as when there is a want of age or understanding, or one of the parties is an idiot or lunatic, or when a prior marriage is still subsisting, the marriage is void absolutely and from the beginning."

Sec. 25. Deaf mutes may contract matrimony, and the engagement may be solemnized by signs. Of course it is no objection to a matrimonial alliance that the parties are blind.

Sec. 26. A third impediment to marriage is the impotence of one or both of the parties, which may be said to be the permanent inability from malformation, accident or disease, for copulation or procreation. This is made a disability by the statutes of most of the states, but as it is an infirmity that cannot be known to the officiating clergyman from ordinary observation, it must be left to the parties in the common-sense manner laid down in the Church of England marriage service, wherein the parties are charged that "marriage is ordained for three purposes: The procreation and education of children; the avoidance of incontinence, and the mutual society, help and comfort of the married pair; and if either of them know any impediment to the lawful joining of the two in matrimony, that they do confess it." Any union where provision is not made for fulfilling all of these purposes may be proved contrary to natural law, using the word in its broadest sense.

Sec. 27. A fourth impediment to marriage is the consanguinity or affinity of the parties. Consanguinity and affinity differ widely in their nature, and yet by the common law little or no distinction is made. In most countries of Europe in which the canon law has had authority or influence, marriages are prohibited between near relatives by blood or marriage. It is very difficult to ascertain the exact point at which the laws of nature have ceased to discountenance the union, and hence the matter is generally regulated by statute; usually the Levitical degrees are adopted as the test of prohibition, and marriages within those degrees, under some exceptions, are made void by statute in many of the states.

Sec. 28. Dr. Taylor, in his Elements of the Civil Law, has gone deeply into the Greek and Roman learning as to the extent of the prohibition of marriage between near relatives, and he says the fourth degree of collateral consanguinity is the proper point to stop at; that the marriage of cousins german, or first cousins, and who are collaterals in the fourth degree, according to the computation of the civilians, and in the second degree according to the canon law, is lawful, and the civil law properly established the fourth as the first degree that could match with decency.

From a great variety of adjudged cases it appears that all marriages related in the ascending or descending line are forbidden, as within the Levitical degrees; but that in the collateral line the prohibition does not extend beyond the third degree of kindred.

Illustrated thus:

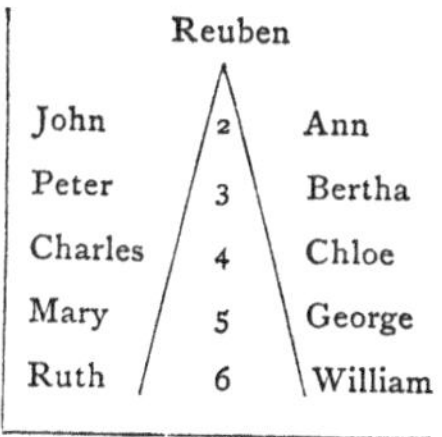

Here John cannot marry Ruth, although four degrees removed, because she is his lineal descendant, nor any in this line. Nor can he marry Ann, because she is his sister and in the second degree of collateral kindred, nor Bertha, because she is in the third degree; but he may marry Chloe, because she is in the fourth degree, computing according to the civil law, as follows: From John to Reuben, the common ancestor in the ascending line, is one, from Reuben to Ann in the descending line is two, from Ann to Bertha is three, from Bertha to Chloe is four. And for the same reason Ann cannot marry William, or any in his line, but she may marry Charles, being in the fourth degree of collateral kindred; and Peter may marry Bertha, being his first cousin and in the fourth degree.

Sec. 29. Whether it be proper or lawful, in a religious or moral sense, for a man to marry his deceased wife's sister, has been discussed at length by American writers. Mr. N. Webster, in his essay published at Boston in 1790, No. 26, held the affirmative. Dr. Livingston, in his dissertation published in New Brunswick in 1816, and confined exclusively to that point, maintained the negative side of the question. The Rev. Dr. S. E. Dwight has also in his Hebrew Wife, a treatise published in 1836, maintained, with much biblical learning and great zeal, that the marriage with a deceased wife's sister was unlawful and incestuous under the Levitical law, and that the biblical law of incest was of general moral obligation, and binding on the whole Gentile world. This is the adjudged law of England, and a marriage between a man and his deceased wife's sister is held to be incestuous.

Sec. 30. It is said that marriage with a sister of a deceased wife is lawful in most of the Protestant states of Europe. In most Catholic countries such marriages are formally prohibited, but dispensations are easily obtained. (See Hayward's Remarks on the Law regarding Marriage with the Sister of a Deceased Wife: London, 1845.) In that pamphlet it is shown, upon very strong reason and authority, that the prohibitions in the Levitical law do not reach the case.

The Rev. Dr. Mathews, of New York, in an able argument in favor of the lawfulness of marrying a deceased wife's sister, delivered before the General Synod of the Reformed Dutch Church, in June, 1843, states that in every state in the Union, except Virginia, such marriages are allowed to be lawful.

Sec. 31. The canon and common law make no distinction between connections by consanguinity and affinity, although the effect upon the offspring is not the same in the one case as the other. Upon this subject, in a leading case in England, the judge observed: "It was necessary in order to perfect the union of marriages, that the husband should take the wife's relatives in the same degree, to be the same as his own, without distinction, and *vice versa;* for if they are to be the same person as was intended by the law of God, they can have no difference in relations, and by consequence the prohibition touching affinity must be carried as far as the prohibition touching consanguinity; for what was found convenient to extinguish jealousies among near relatives, and to govern families and educate children among people of the same consanguinity would likewise have the same operation among those of the same affinity. And when we consider who are prohibited to marry by the Levitical law, we must not only consider the mere words of the law itself, but what, by a just and fair interpretation, may be adduced from it."

Sec. 32. Affinity properly means the tie which arises from marriage between the husband and the blood relations of the wife, and between the wife and the blood relations of the husband; consequently while the marriage remains unbroken the blood relations of the wife stand in the same degree of affinity to the husband as they do in consanguinity to her. Thus the father of the wife stands in the first degree of affinity to his son-in-law as he does in the first degree of consanguinity to his daughter. Relationship by affinity may also exist between the husband and one who is connected by marriage with a blood relation of the wife. Thus, when two men marry sisters, they become related to each other in the second degree of affinity as their wives are related in the second degree of consanguinity. But there is no affinity between the blood relations of the husband and the blood relations of the wife.

Sec. 33. Recently much interest has been elicited in the question whether a man may marry his wife's daughter by a former husband, a case having arisen in Massachusetts; when it was found after such a marriage had taken place between a man of some literary reputation and a daughter of his deceased wife, that the law of that state prohibited such matrimonial alliances; and, doubtless, they are in contravention of the Levitical as well as the common law.

Sec. 34. The marriage of a woman with her husband's son, of course, is in the same degree of affinity. We can easily conceive of a son, under such a loose theory of the law, a possible successor to his father; and a daughter, a candidate for the place of her mother, with the wooing half done at the decease of the parent.

Sec. 35. In 1563 Archbishop Parker published a table of prohibited degrees, which has ever since been regarded the basis of judicial opinion on the subject in England and of legislative enactment in the United States. According to Archbishop Parker's table of degrees a man may not marry his grandmother, grandfather's wife, wife's grandmother, father's sister, mother's sister, father's brother's wife, mother's brother's wife, wife's father's sister, wife's mother's sister, his mother, stepmother, wife's mother, his daughter, wife's daughter, son's wife, his sister, wife's sister, brother's wife, son's daughter, daughter's daughter, son's son's wife, daughter's son's wife, wife's son's daughter, wife's daughter's daughter, brother's daughter, sister's daughter, brother's son's wife, sister's son's wife, wife's brother's daughter, or wife's sister's daughter. And a woman may not marry her grandfather, grandmother's husband, husband's grandfather, father's brother, mother's brother, father's sister's husband, mother's sister's husband, husband's father's brother, husband's mother's brother, her father, stepfather, husband's father, her son, husband's son, daughter's husband, her brother, husband's brother, sister's husband, son's son, daughter's son, son's daughter's husband, daughter's daughter's husband, husband's son's son, husband's daughter's son, brother's son, sister's son, brother's daughter's husband, sister's daughter's husband, husband's brother's son, or husband's sister's son.

Sec. 36. In some countries and states, statutes exist to prevent intermarriages between the white races and people of color, and under the civil law certain persons were prohibited from joining in marriage because of their civil condition. Thus in several of the United States marriages are positively prohibited between the white and colored races. Most of the late slave states had statutes prohibiting intermarriage between free negroes and slaves, but all of those laws have been either repealed or become obsolete, and the interdict of marriages between persons of the white and colored races by statute is becoming more and more uncommon, as experience has shown that the matter may very properly and safely be left to the education, tastes and customs of the people.

Sec. 37. A fifth impediment to marriage is a prior marriage. No person can marry while the former husband or wife is still living. Such second marriage is, by the common law, absolutely null and void, and it is probably an indictable offense in most of the states of the Union, if not all of them. Of course this is subject to the exception that a divorce may have been granted, and in New York and in some other states that divorce must be for some other cause than the adultery of such person proposing to be married.

Sec. 38. Also, in that state and many others, if one of the married parties shall absent himself or herself from the other by the space of five successive years, and the one remarrying shall not know the other who was thus absent to be living within that time, or if the former husband or wife had been sentenced to imprisonment for life, or if the former marriage has been declared void or was made within the age of consent, the former marriage in these excepted cases forms no impediment. It should be stated, however, that in case of the absence of the husband or wife for five years without the knowledge of the other, the marriage will be void only from the time it shall be declared so by a court of competent jurisdiction. And in case of the final sentence of imprisonment for life of one of the parties, no pardon shall have the effect to restore such person to the rights of any previous marriage.

Sec. 39. Under these statutes it has been held that when a man has been divorced for his adultery, and marries again during the life of his former wife, that his last marriage is absolutely void. Many religious organizations have, by rules of discipline, aimed to control their ministers ministering in the solemnization of matrimony. By a canon of the Protestant Episcopal Church in the United States, the ministers of that church are forbidden to solemnize matrimony in any case where there is a divorced wife or husband of either party still living, but the inhibition is not held to apply to the innocent party in a divorce for the cause of adultery, or to parties once divorced seeking to be united again.

Sec. 40. The question now proper to be considered is, what effect the non-observance of the provisions of law regulating marriage will have upon the contract; as we have seen (*supra*) that no marriage can be avoided by reason of the want of any given ceremony in its solemnization unless the statute makes it a prerequisite to a valid marriage. In most states the marriage is held to be valid and binding notwithstanding it is entered into with no rites or ceremonies.

Sec. 41. And it is now equally well settled that a precise compliance with all the requirements of law is never deemed necessary to the validity of the marriage, and that a disregard of some important provisions of the statute may subject the officiating clergyman to a penalty, but will not vitiate the marriage; as in New York it is provided that if the marriage is solemnized contrary to a certain provision of the statute, the minister or magistrate officiating is deemed guilty of a misdemeanor; and in Wisconsin the statute provides that "if any person authorized by law to join persons in marriage shall knowingly solemnize any marriage contrary to these provisions, or willfully make any false certificate of any marriage, shall be punished by fine and imprisonment."

Sec. 42. Many other states have similar statutes, and yet the courts hold that the marriage may be valid without any solemnization at all; that such statutes are intended as directory only upon ministers and magistrates, and to prevent as far as possible, by penalties upon them, the solemnization of marriages when the prescribed conditions and formalities have not been fulfilled.

Sec. 43. In the language of Parsons, Chief Justice: "When a justice or minister shall solemnize a marriage between parties who may lawfully marry, but not without consent of parents or guardians, being under proper age, such consent being wanting, such marriage would unquestionably be lawful, although the officer would incur the penalty for breach of duty." This is certainly reason as well as law; it would entail interminable confusion upon society if marriages were held void on these grounds; the parties to them, generally young and inexperienced persons, have no thought for legal rules or enactments, and it cannot be expected they would have.

Sec. 44. Undoubtedly the weight of authority is in favor of the rule that, in the absence of any provision of law declaring marriages not celebrated in a prescribed manner, or between parties of certain ages, absolutely void, all marriages regularly made according to the common law are valid and binding, although had in violation of the specific regulations imposed by statute. This is the general doctrine of the courts both in this country and in England.

Sec. 45. Of course when a civil government has established regulations for the due celebration of marriages, it is the duty as well as the interest of all the citizens to conform to such regulations; and oftentimes the most serious consequences follow from a failure to comply with the law in regard to marriage, as there may be such an utter disregard of the forms of law that the proof of marriage cannot be made in after years when all the witnesses are dead, no authentic record of the fact having been made.

Sec. 46. In the solemnization of matrimony no particular form is required by the common law, and rarely by the statutes of any of the states, except that the parties shall solemnly declare, in the presence of the minister or magistrate and the attending witnesses, that they take each other as husband and wife. It should not for that reason be supposed that no form need be used, or that ceremony is of no consequence. Marriage is so important a relation, so deeply solemn, and so weighted with consequences that reach to the unseen world, that all civilized and christian people have regarded a formal solemnization as highly proper and useful. That there shall be no uncertainty about it, the laws in many of the old countries, and also some of the states of the Union, require banns to be published before public assemblies, and also sometimes in the public prints, and in others a license; but in all great importance is attached to its proper celebration. The following form may be used in case no other is preferred, and is proper in all the states.

Sec. 47. At the time appointed for the solemnization of matrimony, the persons to be married having presented themselves in the body of the church, or in some other proper place, with the witnesses, and there standing together, the man on the right hand and the woman on the left, and joining hands, the minister may say first to the man:

CEREMONY OF MARRIAGE.

You, G S, now solemnly declare that you take the woman whom you hold by the right hand to be your lawful wedded wife, and you engage to love, cherish and protect her, in sickness and in health, in prosperity and in adversity, and forsaking all others, that you will provide for and support her, and do for her in all things as is commanded by the ordinances of God, and required by the laws of the state, so long as you both do live. Do you on your part thus covenant and promise? *Ans.* I do.

You, C D, now solemnly declare that you take the man whom you hold by the right hand to be your lawful wedded husband, and you engage to love, cherish and obey him, in sickness and in health, in prosperity and in adversity, and forsaking all others, that you will honor, respect and assist him, and do for him in all things as is commanded by the ordinances of

God and required by the laws of the state, so long as you both do live. Do you on your part thus covenant and promise? *Ans.* I do.

Now, therefore, by virtue of the power and authority in me vested, in the presence of God and these witnesses, I pronounce and declare you lawful husband and wife.

A SHORT FORM OF MARRIAGE CEREMONY.

By this act of joining hands you now solemnly declare, in the presence of God and these witnesses, that you take upon yourselves the relation of husband and wife, and solemnly promise and engage to love and honor, comfort and cherish each other as such so long as you both shall live. Therefore, by virtue of the authority in me vested by the laws of the state, I do now pronounce you husband and wife.

Sec. 48. I have in these pages been considering the subject of marriage under the common law, by which is meant that branch of the law of England which does not owe its origin to parliamentary enactments, otherwise called with reference to its origin the unwritten law, as distinguished from statute law, being a collection of customs, rules and maxims which have acquired the force of law by immemorial usage, recognized and declared by judicial decisions, the best evidence of which is to be found in the reports of such decisions and in the standard treatises and abridgments.

Sec. 49. I have also spoken of the canon law, which is somewhat interwoven with it, by which is meant a collection of ecclesiastical constitutions for the regulation of the polity and discipline of the Church of Rome, consisting for the most part of ordinances of general and provincial councils, decrees promulgated by the popes with the sanction of the cardinals, and decretal epistles and bulls of the popes. The canon law of England, composed of legatine or ecclesiastical and provincial constitutions enacted in England prior to the Reformation and adapted to the exigencies of the English church and kingdom. At the time of the Reformation it was provided by statute that a review should be had of the canon law. No such review was, however, perfected, so that the canon law of England remained the same as before the Reformation.

Sec. 50. I have also spoken of the civil law, by which is meant the Roman law, as comprised in the Code, Pandects, Institutes, and Novels of Justinian and his successors, constituting together what is termed the *corpus juris civilis*, as distinguished from the canon and common law.

Sec. 51. I come now to present the statute law under which we live, which is the express written enactments of the legislatures of the several states, to which all other laws must yield.

CHAPTER II.

ILLINOIS STATUTES OF MARRIAGE.

Section 1. Marriages between parents and children, including grandparents and grandchildren of every degree; between brothers and sisters of the half as well as of the whole blood; and between uncles and nieces, aunts and nephews, are declared to be incestuous and void. This section shall extend to illegitimate as well as legitimate children and relatives.

Sec. 2. No insane person or idiot shall be capable of contracting marriage.

Sec. 3. Male persons over the age of seventeen years, and females over the age of fourteen years, may contract and be joined in marriage.

Sec. 4. Marriages may be celebrated either by a minister of the gospel in regular standing in the church or society to which he belongs, by a judge of any court of record, or by a justice of the peace.

Sec. 5. All persons belonging to any religious society, church or denomination may celebrate their marriage according to the rules and principles of such religious society, church or denomination.

Sec. 6. Persons intending to be joined in marriage shall, before their marriage, obtain a license from the county clerk of the county where such marriage is to take place, or shall cause their intention to marry to be published at least two weeks previous to the marriage in the church or congregation to which the parties or one of them belongs.

Sec. 7. The license shall be substantially in the following form:

STATE OF ILLINOIS, } ss.
—— COUNTY, }

Marriage may be celebrated between A B, of ——, in the county of ——, and State of Illinois, of the age of —— years, and C D, of —— in the county of ——, and State of Illinois, of the age of —— years; (*if the man is under the age of twenty-one years, or the woman under eighteen years of age, add the following*) the father (*or mother or guardian, as the case may be*) of the said A B and C D (*or A B or C D, as the case may be*) having given his (*or her*) consent to said marriage.

Witness —— ——, county clerk, and the seal of said county.

Sec. 8. For the purpose of ascertaining the ages of the parties, the county clerk may examine either of them or any other witness under oath.

Sec. 9. The minister, judge or justice of the peace, or if the marriage is celebrated according to the rules and principles of a religious society, church or denomination, and there be no minister, then the clerk or secretary of such society, church or denomination, shall within thirty days after such marriage is solemnized make a certificate thereof and return the same, together with the license if one has been issued, to the clerk of the county in which the marriage took place, or to his successor in office.

Sec. 10. The certificate may be substantially in the following form:

STATE OF ILLINOIS, }
—— COUNTY, } SS.

I, E F, a justice of the peace (*or as the case may be*), hereby certify that A B and C D were united by me in marriage at ——, in the county of ——, and State of Illinois, on the —— day of ——, A.D. 187—.

——.

Sec. 11. The county clerk, upon receiving such certificate, shall make a registry thereof in a book to be kept in his office for that purpose only, which register shall contain the christian and surnames of the parties, the time of their marriage, and the name of the person certifying the same; he shall also at the same time indorse on such certificate the time when the same is registered, and shall number and carefully preserve the same.

Sec. 12. Such certificate, or a copy of the same, or of the entry in such registry certified by the county clerk under the seal of the county, shall be received as evidence of the marriage of the parties as therein stated.

Sec. 13. If any county clerk shall issue a license for the marriage of a man under the age of twenty-one years, or of a woman under the age of eighteen years, without the consent of his or her father (or if he is dead or incapable or not residing with his family, of his or her mother or guardian if he or she have one) first had thereto, he shall forfeit and pay the sum of three hundred dollars for each offense, to be recovered by such father or mother or guardian in an action of debt in any court of competent jurisdiction.

Sec. 14. If any county clerk shall refuse or neglect to register and file any marriage certificate according to law for more than thirty days after the same is returned to him for that purpose (his fees therefor being paid), he shall forfeit and pay one hundred dollars, to be recovered by the party injured in an action of debt in any court of competent jurisdiction.

Sec. 15. If any minister, judge or justice of the peace, or any other officer or person or persons, shall celebrate a marriage without a license having been first obtained therefor as provided by law, he or they shall for every such offense forfeit and pay one hundred dollars, to be recovered in the name of the people of the state in an action of debt in any court of competent jurisdiction: *Provided*, this section shall not apply where the intention of the parties to marry has been published as required in section six of this act.

Sec. 16. If any minister, judge or justice of the peace having celebrated a marriage, or any clerk or secretary of any society, church or denomination among whom a marriage is celebrated, and whose duty it shall be to make and return a certificate of such marriage, shall fail to make and return to the county clerk such certificate in the time and manner provided by law, he shall forfeit and pay one hundred dollars, to be recovered in the name of the people of the State of Illinois in an action of debt in any court of competent jurisdiction.

Sec. 17. It shall be the duty of the state's attorney of the proper county to prosecute all offenses under the two preceding sections.

NOTE.—For forms of marriage ceremony see *ante*, pages 26 and 27.

CHAPTER III.

ILLINOIS STATUTES OF RELIGION AND RELIGIOUS ASSEMBLIES.

ARTICLE II.

CONSTITUTIONAL PROVISIONS.

Section 1. The free exercise and enjoyment of religious profession and worship without discrimination shall forever be guaranteed, and no person shall be denied any civil or political right, privilege or capacity on account of his religious opinions; but the liberty of conscience hereby secured shall not be construed to dispense with oaths or affirmations, excuse acts of licentiousness, or justify practices inconsistent with the peace or safety of the state. No person shall be required to attend or support any ministry or place of worship against his consent, nor shall any preference be given by law to any religious denomination or mode of worship.

ARTICLE VIII.

Sec. 2. Neither the general assembly nor any county, city, town, township, school district, or other public corporation, shall ever make any appropriation, or pay from any public fund whatever, anything in aid of any church or sectarian purpose, or to help support or sustain any school, academy, seminary, college, university, or other literary or scientific institution controlled by any church or sectarian denomination whatever; nor shall any grant or donation of land, money or other personal property ever be made by the state or any such public corporation to any church or for any sectarian purpose.

STATUTES.

Sec. 3. Clergymen of all denominations shall be admitted freely, and without hindrance or restraint, to visit at pleasure any inmate confined in the penitentiary at Joliet, or in any other prison, reformatory or charitable institution belonging to the State of Illinois, subject to such rules and regulations as may be established by the officers in charge of said institutions: *Provided, however*, that the clergyman so applying shall produce to the officers in charge of such institution visited as aforesaid satisfactory evidence from the church authorities to which he belongs, that he is a clergyman in good standing.

Sec. 4. It shall be the duty of the warden, superintendent, or other officer in charge of any institution mentioned in the preceding section of this act, to permit the ministrations of religion according to the rites and ceremonies of the church to which the visiting clergyman belongs, and to aid and assist such of the inmates as aforesaid who may desire it, to the comforts of religion at the hands of a clergyman of his or her own selection.

Sec. 5. Whoever by menace, profane swearing, vulgar language, or any disorderly or unusual conduct, interrupts or disturbs any assembly of people met for the worship of God, shall be fined not exceeding one hundred dollars.

Sec. 6. Whoever during the time of holding any camp or field meeting for religious purposes, and within one mile of the place of holding such meeting, hawks or peddles goods, wares, or merchandise, or without permission of the authorities having charge of such meeting, establishes any tent, booth or other place for vending provisions or refreshments, or sells or gives away, or offers to sell or give away, any spirituous liquors, wine, cider or beer, or practices or engages in gaming or horse racing, or exhibits or offers to exhibit any show or play, shall be fined not exceeding one hundred dollars for each offense: *Provided*, that whoever has his regular place of business within such limits is not hereby required to suspend his business.

CHAPTER IV.

ILLINOIS STATUTES OF RELIGIOUS SOCIETIES.

Section 1. Any church, congregation or society formed for the purpose of religious worship, may become incorporated in the manner following, to wit: By electing or appointing, according to its usages or customs, at any meeting held for that purpose, two or more of its members as trustees, wardens and vestrymen, or such other officers whose powers and duties are similar to those of trustees, as shall be agreeable to the usages and customs, rules or regulations of such congregation, church or society, and may adopt a corporate name, and upon the filing of the affidavit as hereinafter provided it shall be and remain a body politic and corporate by the name so adopted.

Sec. 2. The chairman or secretary of such meeting shall, as soon as may be after such meeting, make and file in the office of recorder of deeds in the county in which such congregation, church or society is organized (which shall be recorded by such recorder), an affidavit substantially in the following form:

STATE OF ILLINOIS, }
—— COUNTY, } SS.

I do solemnly swear (*or affirm, as the case may be*) that at a meeting of the members of the (*here insert the name of the church, society or congregation, as known before incorporation*), held at (*here insert the place of meeting*) in the county of ——, and State of Illinois, on the —— day of ——, A.D. 187—, for that purpose, the following persons were elected (*or appointed*) (*here insert their names*) trustees (*or wardens, vestrymen or officers, by whatever name they choose to adopt with powers and duties similar to trustees*) according to the rules and usages of (*such church, society or congregation*); and said (*church, society or congregation*) adopted as its corporate name (*here insert the name*); and at said meeting this affiant acted as (*chairman, or secretary, as the case may be*).

(Name of affiant.)

Subscribed and sworn to before me this —— day of ——, A.D. 18—. —— ——,

Clerk of Court.

Such affidavit or copy thereof, duly certified by the recorder, shall be received as evidence of the due incorporation of such congregation, church or society.

Sec. 3. The term of office of the trustees of any such corporation may be determined by the rules or by-laws of the congregation, church or society.

Sec. 4. A failure to elect trustees at any time shall not work a dissolution of such corporation, but the trustees last elected shall be considered as in office until their successors are elected.

Sec. 5. All elections of trustees after the first, and elections to fill vacancies, may be called and conducted upon such notice and in such manner as may be provided by the rules, usages or by-laws of the congregation, church or society, but the qualification and number of the trustees shall, at all times, be the same as required in the first section of this act. No certificate of election after the first need be filed for record.

Sec. 6. A trustee may be removed from office by an election called and conducted in like manner as elections for trustees, or his office declared vacant by failure to act, immoral conduct, or for an abandonment of the faith of the congregation, church or society.

Sec. 7. Upon the incorporation of any congregation, church, or society, all real and personal property held by any person or trustees, for the use of the members thereof, shall immediately vest in such corporation and be subject to its control, and may be used, mortgaged, sold and conveyed, the same as if it had been conveyed to such corporation by deed, but no such conveyance or mortgage shall be made so as to affect or destroy the intent or effect of any grant, devise or donation that may be made to such person or trustees for the use of such congregation, church or society.

Sec. 8. Any corporation that may be formed for religious purposes under this act, or under any law of this state for the incorporation of religious societies, may receive by gift, devise or purchase, land not exceeding in quantity (including that already held by such corporation) ten acres, and may erect or build thereon such house, buildings or other improvements as it may deem necessary for the convenience and comfort of such congregation, church or society, and may lay out and maintain thereon a burying-ground; but no such property shall be used except in the manner expressed in the gift, grant or devise, or if no use or trust is so expressed, except for the benefit of the congregation, church or society for which it was intended.

Sec. 9. The trustees shall have the care, custody and control of the real and personal property of the corporation, subject to the direction of the congregation, church or society, and may, when directed by the congregation, church or society, erect houses or buildings and improvements, and repair and alter the same, and may, when so directed, mortgage, encumber, sell and convey all real or personal estate of such corporation: *Provided*, that no mortgage, encumbrance, sale or conveyance shall be made of any such estate so as to defeat or destroy the effect of any gift, grant, devise or bequest which may be made to such corporation, but all such gifts, grants, devises and bequests shall be appropriated and used as directed or intended by the person or persons making the same.

Sec. 10. Any congregation, church or society heretofore incorporated under the provisions of any law for the incorporation of religious societies, may become incorporated under the provisions of this act relative to religious societies in the same manner as if it had not previously been incorporated; in which case the new corporation shall be entitled to and invested with all the real and personal estate of the old corporation, in like manner and to the same extent as the old corporation, subject to all the debts, contracts and liabilities. The word trustees, wherever used in this act, shall be construed to include wardens and vestrymen, or such other officers as perform the duties of trustees.

Sec. 11. Any congregation, church or society incorporated under this act, may receive by grant, devise or bequest, real estate not exceeding forty acres, for the purpose of holding camp-meetings, and may put such improvements thereon as they may deem for their comfort and convenience. The title to such real estate shall be in such corporation, subject to like conditions as are provided in this act in regard to other real estate held by such corporation.

Sec. 12. The trustees or any other persons designated by any such congregation, church or society incorporated under this act, shall have power to publish, print, circulate, sell or give away such religious, Sabbath-school and missionary tracts, periodicals or books as they may deem necessary to the promotion of religion and morality.

PROPERTY EXEMPT FROM TAXATION.

Scc. 13. All church property actually and exclusively used for public worship, when the land (to be of reasonable size for the location of the church building) is owned by the congregation.

CHAPTER V.

INDIANA STATUTES OF MARRIAGE.

Section 1. Marriage is declared to be a civil contract, into which males of the age of seventeen and females of the age of fourteen, not within the prohibited degrees of consanguinity, are capable of entering.

Sec. 2. The following marriages are declared void:

1. When either party has a wife or husband living at the time of such marriage.

2. When one of the parties is a white person and the other possessed of one eighth or more of negro blood.

3. When either party is insane or idiotic at the time of such marriage.

Sec. 3. Marriages may be solemnized by ministers of the gospel and priests of every church throughout the state, judges of courts of record, and justices of the peace within their respective counties, and by the Society of Friends and German Baptists according to the rules of their societies: *Provided*, that no marriage legal in other respects shall be void on account of the incapacity of the person solemnizing the same.

Sec. 4. Before any persons, except members of the Society of Friends, shall be joined in marriage, they shall produce a license from the clerk of the circuit court of the county in which the female resides, directed to any person empowered by law to solemnize marriages, and authorizing him to join together the persons therein named as husband and wife.

NOTE.—The clerk of one county cannot issue license for the marriage of a female who is a resident of another county. But the license, if properly issued, will authorize the solemnization of the marriage in any county in the state.

Sec. 5. Such license shall not be issued by the clerk without the consent of the parent or guardian, if there be any, if the female be within the age of eighteen or the male within the age of twenty-one. When there is no parent or guardian resident within the state, and the female has resided within the county where license is sought to be obtained for one month preceding such application, license may issue.

Sec. 6. An affidavit of the facts as required to exist by the last preceding section, made by some disintèrested person, shall be a sufficient justification of the clerk in issuing any license.

Sec. 7. No marriage shall be void or voidable for want of license or other formality required by law, if either of the parties thereto believed it to be legal marriage at the time.

Sec. 8. Every person who shall solemnize any marriage by virtue of the provisions of this act shall, within three months thereafter, file a certificate thereof in the clerk's office of the county in which such marriage was solemnized, which certificate shall, by such clerk, be recorded, together with such license, and such record or a copy thereof, shall be presumptive evidence of the facts therein stated.

NOTE.— FORM OF CERTIFICATE.

This is to certify that Mr. A B, of ——, in the county of —— and State of ——, and Miss E R, a resident of ——, in the county of —— and State or Indiana, were joined in holy matrimony by me at ——, in the State of Indiana, on the —— day of ——, in the year of our Lord one thousand eight hundred and ——. The said A B having produced to me the license required by law, issued by the clerk of the circuit court of the county of ——, being the county where the said E R, the female, resided at the time such marriage took place, and there appearing to be no legal impediment thereto.

Witness my hand this —— day of ——, 18—.

—— ——,
Rector (*or Pastor*) of —— Church.

Sec. 9. Relates to duties of clerks.

Sec. 10. If any person empowered to solemnize marriage shall join any persons in marriage contrary to the provisions of this act, he shall, upon conviction thereof, be fined in any sum not exceeding five hundred dollars.

Sec. 11. Any person solemnizing a marriage, who shall fail to return a certificate thereof within the time prescribed by law, shall be fined not less than five nor more than one hundred dollars.

Sec. 12. If any person having solemnized a marriage shall fail to file a certificate thereof in the proper clerk's office as in this act required, he shall, upon conviction thereof, be fined the sum of five dollars for every month he shall continue to fail or neglect to file such certificate, from and after the expiration of the time within which he is required by this act to file the same.

Sec. 13. If any person shall undertake to join others in marriage knowing that he is not lawfully authorized so to do, he shall, upon conviction thereof, be fined in any sum not less than fifty nor more than five hundred dollars, to which may be added imprisonment in the county jail for a term not exceeding three months.

Sec. 14. Every person who shall knowingly counsel or assist in any manner in any marriage between any person having one eighth part or more of negro blood and any white person, shall be fined not less than one hundred nor more than one thousand dollars.

NOTE.—For ceremony of marriage see *ante*, pages 26 and 27.

CHAPTER VI.

INDIANA STATUTES OF RELIGIOUS SOCIETIES.

Section 1. The wardens and vestrymen of any parish or congregation of any church in this state, duly chosen according to the provisions of this act, in accordance with the rules and usages of said church, after a record of such election shall have been made as herein provided, shall be deemed a body corporate and politic under the name of wardens and vestrymen of —— church ——, and by such name shall have power to contract and be contracted with, sue and be sued, with the like effect as other persons and corporations.

Sec. 2. The number to be elected under the provisions of this act shall not be less than three nor more than nine; but the rector of any parish church or congregation shall be *ex-officio* a member of the vestry of the same, according to the rules, regulations and form of government of the church; and the members of the vestry so elected shall severally hold their offices until their successors are duly chosen according to the rules and usages of said church.

Sec. 3. At the first and every subsequent election, the officers appointed to take count and make a full list of the votes given shall within ten days thereafter deposit in the recorder's office of the proper county a certificate setting forth the notice of such election, the time and place where the same was held, and the name of the persons elected; and the recorder of such county shall immediately make a proper record of the same.

NOTE.—CERTIFICATE OF ELECTION AND INCORPORATION.

To all to whom these presents may come:

We whose names are hereunto subscribed, appointed to take count and make a full list of the votes given at an election of wardens and vestrymen of —— Church, do hereby certify that on the —— day of ——, in the year 18—, the male persons of full age worshiping in the church (*or schoolhouse, as the case may be*) in the town of ——, county of ——, and State of Indiana, in which congregation divine worship is celebrated according to the rites of the Protestant Episcopal Church in the State of Indiana, and which is not already incorporated, met at their place of worship (*or at the house of A K*) for the purpose of incorporating themselves under the laws of the State of Indiana, and in pursuance of notice duly given to the said congregation at the time of morning service on two Sundays previous (*or three days previous*) that a meeting would be held on Monday in Easter week (*or on the —— day of ——, 18—*), at 10 o'clock A.M., at their place of worship in the town of ——, county of ——, for the purpose of incorporating themselves and of electing two church-wardens and eight vestrymen (*not less than three nor more than nine*). And we further certify that the Rev. A B, being rector of said church (*or if there be no rector, say the undersigned L M was by a majority vote of the members of said congregation called to the chair and*) presided at said meeting. And we further certify that at said meeting C D and E F were duly elected wardens of said church, and O P, S T, etc., were duly elected vestrymen; that Tuesday in Easter week (*or as the case may be*) was by the said meeting fixed as the day on which the term of office of said church-wardens and vestrymen should annually thereafter cease and their successors be chosen. And said meeting determined and declared by a majority vote that the said church and congregation should be known in the law by the name of the Rector, Wardens and Vestrymen of (*St. John's Church*), of the town or city of ——, in the county of ——.

In testimony whereof we, the said A B, Rector (*or L M, who presided at said meeting*), and R F, S T, who were appointed to take count and make a full list of the votes given at such election, have hereunto subscribed our names and affixed our seals this —— day of ——, in the year of our Lord one thousand eight hundred and ——.

Signed and sealed in presence of —— ——.
A B, Rector. [SEAL]
R F. [SEAL]
S T. [SEAL]
J Y. [SEAL]

CERTIFICATE OF ELECTION OF OFFICERS TO BE FILED ANNUALLY.

To all to whom these presents may come:

We whose names are hereunto subscribed, being appointed to take count and make a full list of the votes given at the annual election of wardens and vestrymen of (*St. John's Church*) for the ensuing year, do hereby certify that notice of an election of wardens and vestrymen of said church was given to the congregation at the morning service on Sunday, the —— day of ——, 18—, by the announcement of the rector of such election to take place at the church on Easter Monday, in the year 18—, at 10 o'clock in the forenoon. That said election was duly held at the time and place mentioned in said notice, at which the Rev. A B, rector of said church, occupied the chair and presided at said meeting, and that the undersigned R F and S T were appointed to take count and make a full list of the votes given at said election. That C D and E F were duly elected church-wardens and O P, S T, etc., were duly elected vestrymen of said church for the ensuing year.

In testimony whereof we have hereunto set our hands and seals this —— day of ——, 18—.
A B, Rector. [SEAL]
R F. [SEAL]
S T. [SEAL]

NOTE.—It is of the highest importance that all the provisions of the statute be complied with in the incorporation of a church or religious society, as a neglect of any of its provisions would deprive it of a legal existence, and all its acts would be void.

Sec. 4. When any person so elected shall refuse to serve, or shall die, resign or be removed from office, the remaining members of the vestry in which such vacancy may occur shall be authorized to appoint another person to fill the vacancy until the next regular election.

Sec. 5. The peculiar name of any church, parish or congregation may be altered or changed, as also the number of the members of any vestry, so that the number be not made more nor less than the number specified in this act; but the name chosen under the provisions of this section shall not be assumed until a record has first been made of the fact in the recorder's office of the proper county. Such change shall not affect the rights or liabilities of the vestry, parish or congregation, or of other persons or parties.

Sec. 6. The wardens and vestrymen of any church, parish or congregation may establish by-laws to carry out the objects of their organization; they shall have power to receive conveyances of lots or lands by purchase, gift or otherwise, not exceeding one hundred acres, and to hold the same to their successors in perpetuity for the sole and exclusive benefit of such church, parish or congregation, and for the uses declared in such conveyance or grant; they may erect and hold buildings for religious worship, for parsonages or for educational or benevolent purposes; they may lay out and establish suitable grounds for a cemetery or place for the burial of the dead, and after the plat thereof shall have been duly recorded in the recorder's office of the proper county, they shall enjoy all the privileges necessary for the preservation and protection of such cemetery; and they may appoint trustees or committees to take charge of any school, hospital or cemetery which they may establish, and give direction concerning the management of the same: *Provided, however*, that such appointment shall not relieve or release such vestry, parish or congregation from any legal liability to which they may be subject.

Sec. 7. Such vestry and their successors in office may also acquire and possess for the use of any such parish, church or congregation, personal property not exceeding in value the sum of five thousand dollars, and may appropriate the same and the income or interest thereof and all other funds and incomes in their hands, as such vestry to the maintenance of religious worship, schools, libraries, or other purposes not inconsistent with the trust.

Sec. 8. Such vestry, to more effectually carry out the object of this trust, may sell, lease or otherwise dispose of their corporate property; and any conveyance thereof by such vestry or a majority of them, in behalf of such church, parish or congregation, shall vest in the purchaser of the same all the right, title and interest thereto; but the provisions of this section shall not be construed to affect any gift, bequest or devise to such parish, church or congregation, or to the vestry thereof for its use, nor to defeat the intentions of the grantor, donor or testator.

Sec. 9. As between such parish, church or congregation, the vestry thereof, and all persons claiming under them, and any person granting real estate thereto, and all persons claiming under him, the certificate of election provided for in the third section of this act, shall be conclusive evidence of the matters and things therein recited; and as between such parish, church or congregation, the vestry thereof and all persons claiming under them, and all other persons, it shall be presumptive evidence of such matters.

Sec. 10. Whenever any parish, church or congregation shall have elected a vestry in conformity to the provisions of this act, and the same shall have been dissolved by the death, resignation or removal of its members, a majority of persons entitled to vote may, within five years after such dissolution, proceed to elect a new vestry in conformity with the provisions herein contained; and such new vestry, after a record of the election shall have been made, as required in the third section of this act, shall have the same powers, and may do and perform all other acts and things which by the provisions of this law a vestry may do and perform.

UNION OF TWO OR MORE CHURCHES.

Sec. 11. When the members of two or more churches desire to form a union and assume a new name, be and they are hereby authorized so to do, by each church appointing three of its members as trustees, who shall within twenty days after their appointment meet at a time and place agreed upon, and regularly organize by appointing one of their number chairman and another secretary of their meeting, and when so organized they shall agree upon the name that the united church shall thereafter assume.

Sec. 12. The secretary shall record the proceedings of said meeting in a record to be kept for that purpose, and shall within ten days thereafter deposit in the recorder's office of the county where said church shall hold its place of worship, a certificate setting forth the names of the old churches that have united, the name of the new church, and the names of the trustees thereof, and the recorder shall record the same among the records of deeds in his office.

NOTE.— FORM OF CERTIFICATE OF UNION.

To all to whom these presents shall come:

I hereby certify that at a meeting of the members of the church (*or society*) heretofore known as —— ——, held at their house of worship (*or at the house of A B*), in the town of ——, county of ——, State of Indiana, on the —— day of ——, 18—, the following named persons were chosen as trustees, viz., N O, R S, and W L. That a meeting of the members of the church (*or society*) heretofore known as the —— ——, held at their house of worship (*or at the house of A B*), in said town of ——, county of ——, and state aforesaid, on the —— day of ——, 18—, the following persons, members of said church (*or society*) were appointed trustees thereof, viz., S T, M R, and S H, in pursuance of the statute providing for the union of two or more churches. That the trustees so appointed by the two churches above named for the purpose of forming a union, did meet at the church of —— (*or at the house of A B*), in the said town of ——, county of ——, State of Indiana, on the —— day of ——, 18—, at 9 o'clock A.M., being within twenty days after their said appointment, and did regularly organize by the appointment of N O, one of their number, chairman, and the undersigned R S secretary of the said meeting. After such organization the said trustees so assembled did agree by a majority vote that the united church should assume the name of —— ——, and by said name should ever thereafter be called and known.

In testimony whereof I have hereunto set my hand and seal this —— day of ——, 18—.

——, Secretary. [SEAL]

Sec. 13. Said trustees so appointed shall be the trustees of said new church until their successors shall be duly elected and qualified, and shall be deemed a body politic and corporate by the name and style of the "Trustees of——," and by that name shall have power to contract and be contracted with, sue and be sued, to receive and dispose of real and personal estate for the sole use and benefit of said new church, in like manner and with like effect as other persons or corporations.

Sec. 14. After said certificate is recorded in the recorder's office, as provided in section twelve of this act, it shall be lawful for the trustees of said churches that have united to convey by deed to the trustees of the new church, and their successors in office, all lands belonging to said old churches, which deeds shall be recorded in the recorder's office where said lands are situate, and also to deliver to said trustees of said new church all articles of personal property belonging to said old churches. A list of the articles of personal property so delivered shall be recorded by the secretary of said new church, in the church record as aforesaid, which articles of personal property and real estate shall be held by said trustees of new church and their successors in office for the use and benefit of said new church.

Sec. 15. So soon as the trustees of said old churches shall have made said conveyance of lands and delivery of personal property, as aforesaid, to said trustees of new church, said old churches from and after that time shall cease to exist; and all rights, powers, privileges and liabilities belonging thereto shall, from and after that time, vest in and attach to the new church so organized as aforesaid, with full power to the trustees thereof to sue and be sued, the same as the trustees of the old churches could before they ceased to exist.

Sec. 16. Such new church, when organized as aforesaid, shall have full power to establish all necessary by-laws, and make all needful regulations, to carry out the objects of its organization.

Sec. 17. Such new church may appoint, or elect, a treasurer and such other officers as it may see fit to carry on its organization.

ORGANIZATION OF RELIGIOUS SOCIETIES.

Sec. 18. The members of any church or religious society of any denomination whatever may, after giving ten days' notice, by posting up written or printed notices in three public places in the vicinity of the place where such church or society usually meets for worship, specifying the time and place of such election, or appointment, at any regular or called meeting of such church or society, elect or appoint, according to the usages or customs of such society, not less than three nor more than nine trustees, who shall be a body politic or corporate, by such name as such society may elect and designate for any educational, benevolent or charitable purposes.

NOTE.— FORM OF NOTICE.

Take notice that at a regular (*or called*) meeting of the members of —— church (*or society*) of ——, to be held at their place of public worship (*or at the dwelling-house of A B*), in the town of ——, county of ——, and State of Indiana, on the —— day of ——, 18—, at 7 o'clock P.M. of that day, will be elected trustees for said church (*or society*) according to the usages or custom of said society (*not less than three nor more than nine in number*), as shall be determined at such meeting.

Dated this —— day of ——, 18—. —— ——, Clerk.

Sec. 19. The clerk of such society shall issue to such trustees a certificate setting forth that they have been elected, or appointed, for such purpose, which certificate shall, within twenty days from its date, be recorded among the miscellaneous records of the county in which such election, or appointment, is made; and from the date of such recording said trustees shall be deemed a body politic and corporate, by such name as may have been designated by such society; and as such may sue and be sued, contract and be contracted with, and shall have authority to receive conveyances of land, not exceeding twenty acres, by purchase, devise or gift, and hold the same to them and their successors in perpetuity, for the sole and exclusive uses and purposes of carrying out the objects of such corporate body.

FORM OF CERTIFICATE OF ELECTION.

To A B, C D and E F: I hereby certify that at a regular (*or called*) meeting of the —— church (*or society*) of ——, held at their place of public worship (*or at the dwelling-house of A B*) in the town of ——, county of ——, and State of Indiana, on the evening of the —— day of ——, 18—, you, and each of you, were duly elected trustees of the said church, or society; that notice of such election was duly given by written notices posted up in three public places, to wit: (*here state the places where posted*) ten days previous to such election, stating the time and place at which such election would take place.

Given under my hand this —— day of ——, 18—.

—— ——, Clerk.

Sec. 20. And such corporation shall have power and authority to acquire and possess for the uses and purposes and furtherance of the objects of the same, moneys and personal property, by bequest, donation or otherwise, to any amount not exceeding one hundred thousand dollars, and may appropriate the same, and the income or interest thereof, and all other funds in their hands, for the purposes designated by such society, not inconsistent with their trust nor inconsistent with the conditions of any devise, bequest or donation made to them.

Sec. 21. Such trustees are empowered to sell, loan or otherwise dispose of their corporate property, but not in any manner inconsistent with the duties or objects of their trust.

Sec. 22. Such trustees shall procure a corporate seal.

Sec. 23. Such trustees shall at their first meeting elect one of their number president, another secretary, and another treasurer, and shall procure a well-bound book of not less than three hundred pages, in which shall be kept accurate minutes of their proceedings.

Sec. 24. Such church or religious society shall at the time of election or appointment of such trustees elect or appoint one of them to serve one year, one of them two years, and the other three years from the date of their appointment, and said society shall each year elect or appoint a trustee to succeed the one whose term expires, and may also at any regular meeting of such society elect or appoint a trustee to fill any vacancy that may occur in said board of trustees by death, resignation or otherwise.

Sec. 25. Should there be from any cause a failure to elect or appoint a new trustee as required, those in office shall continue to hold until successors are properly elected or appointed.

Sec. 26. The treasurer of such board of trustees shall give bond with freehold security, to be approved by the president of the board, payable to the State of Indiana, in a sum not less than double the amount of moneys at any time in his hands, conditioned for the faithful and honest discharge of the duties of his trust; and in case of breach of said bond any member of the society electing or appointing such trustees may maintain an action upon said bond as relator, the money recovered thereon to be paid to said corporate body.

Sec. 27. Such board of trustees are empowered to make such by-laws and rules as may be necessary to carry out the objects of their trust.

NOTE.—The foregoing chapter provides for three kinds of church organizations:

1. Sections 1 to 10 inclusive provide for the organization of Protestant Episcopal churches so as to become corporate bodies.
2. Sections 11 to 17 inclusive, for the union of two or more churches under a new name.
3. The remainder of the chapter provides for the organization by the members of any church, religious society or denomination, so as to become a body politic and corporate, possessing all the powers and privileges of a corporation.

CHAPTER VII.

INDIANA STATUTES OF RELIGIOUS ASSEMBLIES.

Section 1. If any person shall disturb any religious society or any member thereof, when met or meeting together for public worship, or shall sell or give away any spirituous liquor at any booth, wagon, shed or open place, or in any building temporarily erected for the purpose of selling therein such liquors, within two miles of any collection of a portion of the citizens of this state convened for the purpose of worship, or shall disturb any collection of the people convened for any lawful purpose, such person shall be fined not exceeding fifty nor less than five dollars, and imprisonment not exceeding thirty days may be added.

Sec. 2. If any person shall erect, bring, keep, continue or maintain any booth, tent, wagon, huckster-shop or other place for the sale of intoxicating liquors, cider, beer or other drinks, or for the sale of any other article whatever; or shall sell or give away any intoxicating liquors, cider, beer or other drinks, or any other article whatever; or shall keep or exhibit any gaming table, roulette, shuffle-board, faro-bank, nine-pin or ten-pin alley, or billiard table, or any other gaming or wagering apparatus whereby any money or article of value may be lost or won; or any person who may be the owner or proprietor of any real property, who shall rent or permit the same to be occupied for any such purpose within one mile of any collection of any inhabitants of this state met together for worship, or any agricultural fair or exhibition, or who shall in any way interrupt, molest or disturb such religious meeting or agricultural fair or exhibition, or any person present thereat or going to or returning therefrom, or who shall molest or disturb any meeting of inhabitants of this state met together for any lawful purpose, shall be fined in any sum not more than twenty-five dollars nor less than five dollars.

Sec. 3. If any person of the age of fourteen years and upward shall be found on the first day of the week, commonly called Sunday, rioting, hunting, fishing, quarreling, at common labor, or engaged in their usual avocations, works of charity and necessity only excepted, such person shall be fined in any sum not less than one nor more than ten dollars; but nothing herein contained shall be construed to affect such as conscientiously observe the seventh day of the week as the Sabbath, travelers, families removing, keepers of toll-bridges and toll-gates, and ferrymen, acting as such.

Sec. 4. No clergyman or priest shall be allowed, in giving testimony, to disclose any communication intrusted to him in his professional capacity, and necessary and proper to enable him to discharge the duties of his profession according to the usual course of practice or discipline, unless with the consent of the party in whose favor the foregoing provisions are enacted.

Sec. 5. All persons going to or returning from any election, place of religious worship, or attending a funeral, shall be exempt from paying toll for crossing any of the toll-bridges contemplated in the act relating to bridges.

Sec. 6. No plank-road company shall charge toll to ministers of the gospel going and returning from their appointments for preaching.

Sec. 7. The following property shall be exempt from taxation: Every building erected for religious worship and the pews and furniture within the same, and the land whereon such building is situate, not exceeding ten acres.

Sec. 8. The following are provisions of the constitution of the state:

ARTICLE I.

Sec. 2. All men shall be secured in their natural right to worship Almighty God according to the dictates of their own consciences.

Sec. 3. No law shall in any case whatever control the free exercise and enjoyment of religious opinions or interfere with the rights of conscience.

Sec. 4. No preference shall be given by law to any creed, religious society or mode of worship; and no man shall be compelled to attend, erect or support any place of worship, or to maintain any ministry against his consent.

Sec. 5. No religious test shall be required as a qualification for any office of trust or profit.

Sec. 6. No money shall be drawn from the treasury for the benefit of any religious or theological institution.

Sec. 7. No person shall be rendered imcompetent as a witness in consequence of his opinions upon matters of religion.

CHAPTER VIII.

IOWA STATUTES OF MARRIAGE.

Section 1. Marriage is a civil contract, requiring the consent of parties capable of entering into other contracts, except as herein otherwise declared.

Sec. 2. A marriage between a male person of sixteen and a female of fourteen years of age is valid, but if either party has not attained the age thus fixed, the marriage is a nullity or not, at the option of such party made known at any time before he or she is six months older than the age thus fixed.

Sec. 3. Previous to any marriage within this state, a license for that purpose must be obtained from the clerk of the circuit court of the county wherein the marriage is to be solemnized, agreeable to the provisions of this chapter.

Sec. 4. Such license must not in any case be granted where either party is under the age necessary to render the marriage absolutely valid; nor shall it be granted where either party is a minor, without the previous consent of the parent or guardian of such minor, nor where the condition of either party is such as to disqualify him for making any other civil contract.

Sec. 5. Unless such clerk is acquainted with the age

and condition of the parties for the marriage of whom the license is applied for he must take the testimony of competent and disinterested witnesses on the subject.

Sec. 6. He must cause due entry of the application for the issuing of the license to be made in a book, to be procured and kept for that purpose, stating that he was acquainted with the parties, and knew them to be of competent age and condition, or that the requisite proof of such fact was made to him by one or more witnesses, stating their names, which book shall constitute a part of the records of his office.

Sec. 7. If either party is a minor, the consent of the parent or guardian must be filed in the clerk's office, after being acknowledged by the said parent or guardian or proved to be genuine, and a memorandum of such facts must also be entered in said book.

Sec. 8. If the clerk of the circuit court grants a license contrary to the provisions of the preceding sections, he is guilty of a misdemeanor; and if a marriage is solemnized without such license being procured, the parties so married, and all persons aiding in such marriage, are likewise guilty of a misdemeanor.

Sec. 9. Marriages must be solemnized either, (1) by a justice of the peace or mayor of the city wherein the marriage takes place; (2) by some judge of the supreme, district or circuit court of this state; or (3) by some officiating minister of the gospel, ordained or licensed according to the usages of his denomination.

Sec. 10. After the marriage has been solemnized, the officiating minister or magistrate shall, on request, give each of the parties a certificate thereof.

FORM OF MARRIAGE CERTIFICATE.

STATE OF IOWA, }
COUNTY OF —— }

I hereby certify that on the —— day of ——, 18—, at the house of T D, Esq. (*or at* —— *Church*), in the *town* (*city or village*) *of* ——, in the county of ——, and State of Iowa, Mr. A B, of ——, and Miss E D, of ——, were with their mutual consent lawfully joined together in holy matrimony, which was solemnized by me in presence of M P, of ——, etc., and R F, attending witnesses.

And I further certify that Mr. A B produced to me the proper marriage license, issued under the hand and seal of P D, clerk of the circuit court for said county, in due form.

Given under my hand this —— day of ——, 18—.

—— ——,

Rector (*or Pastor*) of —— Church.

Sec. 11. Marriages solemnized with the consent of parties in any other manner than is herein prescribed are valid, but the parties themselves, and all other persons aiding or abetting, shall forfeit to the school fund the sum of fifty dollars each.

Sec. 12. The person solemnizing marriage shall forfeit a like amount, unless within ninety days after the ceremony he make return thereof to the clerk of the circuit court.

NOTE.—The return to the clerk of the circuit court may be the same as the certificate given the parties.

Sec. 13. The clerk of the circuit court shall keep a register containing the names of the parties, the date of the marriage, and the name of the person by whom the marriage was solemnized, which, or a certified transcript therefrom, is receivable in all courts and places as evidence of the marriage and the date thereof.

Sec. 14. The provisions of this chapter, so far as they relate to procuring licenses and to the solemnizing of marriages, are not applicable to members of any particular denomination having, as such, any peculiar mode of entering the marriage relation.

Sec. 15. But where any mode is thus pursued which dispenses with the services of a clergyman or magistrate, the husband is responsible for the return directed to be made to the clerk, and is liable to the above named penalty if the return is not made.

Sec. 16. Illegitimate children become legitimate by the subsequent marriage of their parents.

Sec. 17. Marriages between persons whose marriage is prohibited by law, or who have a husband or wife living, are void; but if the parties live and cohabit together after the death of the former husband or wife, such marriage shall be deemed valid.

NOTE.—For marriage ceremony see *ante*, pages 26 and 27.

CHAPTER IX.

IOWA STATUTES OF INCORPORATION OF RELIGIOUS SOCIETIES.

Section 1. Any three or more persons of full age, citizens of the United States, a majority of whom shall be citizens of this state, who desire to associate themselves for benevolent, charitable, scientific, religious or missionary purposes, may make, sign and acknowledge before any officer authorized to take the acknowledgments of deeds in this state, and have recorded in the office of the recorder of the county in which the business of such society is to be conducted, a certificate in writing in which shall be stated the name or title by which such society shall be known, the particular business and objects of such society, the number of trustees, directors or managers to conduct the same, and the names of the trustees, directors or managers of such society for the first year of its existence.

FORM OF CERTIFICATE.

Know all men by these presents, That we, A B, C D, E F, (*not less than three*) of full age, citizens of the United States, and a majority of whom are citizens of the State of Iowa, whose names are hereto subscribed, being desirous to associate ourselves together for religious (*or missionary*) purposes, do now execute and acknowledge these articles of association by which we have agreed and hereby do agree to become incorporated in a religious (*or missionary*) society in pursuance of the laws of this state, by the name or title of the (*here give name in full*), by which such society shall be known and called. That the particular business and objects of said society are (*here state the business and object of the society*). That the number of trustees (*directors or managers*) of said society for the first year shall be (*state number*). And we hereby agree that all persons that shall become hereafter associated with us in this organization shall be entitled to equal rights and privileges with us and to the grants and franchises hereby secured under and by virtue of the statutes in such case made and provided.

In witness whereof we have hereunto set our hands and seals this —— day of ——, 18—.

A B. [SEAL]
C D. [SEAL]
E F. [SEAL]

NOTE.—For form of acknowledgment see *post*, page 125.

Sec. 2. Upon filing for record the certificate as aforesaid, the persons who shall have signed and acknowledged such certificate, and their associates and successors, shall by virtue hereof be a body politic and corporate by the name stated in such certificate, and by that they and their successors shall and may have succession, and shall be persons capable of suing and being sued, and may have and use a common seal, which they may alter or change at pleasure, and they and their successors by their corporate name shall be capable of taking, receiving, purchasing and holding real and personal estate, and of making by-laws for the management of its affairs not inconsistent with law.

Sec. 3. The society so incorporated may annually or oftener elect from its members its trustees, directors or managers, at such time and place and in such manner as may be specified in its by-laws, who shall have the control and management of the affairs and funds of the society, a majority of whom shall be a quorum for the transaction of business; and whenever any vacancy shall happen among such trustees, directors or managers by death, resignation or neglect to serve, such vacancy shall be filled in such manner as shall be provided by the by-laws of such society. When the body corporate consists of the trustees, directors or managers of any benevolent, charitable, literary, scientific, religious or missionary institution, which is or may be established in this state, and which is or may be under the patronage, control, direction or supervision of any synod, conference, association or other ecclesiastical body in such state, established agreeably to the laws thereof, such ecclesiastical body may nominate and appoint such trustees, directors or managers according to usages of the appointing body, and may fill any vacancy which may occur among such trustees, directors or managers; and when any such institution may be under the patronage, control or direction or supervision of two or more of such synods, conferences, associations or other ecclesiastical bodies, such bodies may severally nominate and appoint such proportion of such trustees, directors or managers as shall be agreed upon by those bodies immediately concerned. And any vacancy occurring among such appointees last named shall be filled by the synod, conference, association or body having appointed the last incumbent.

Sec. 4. Any corporation in this state of an academical character, the memberships of which shall consist of lay members and pastors of churches delegates to any synod, conference or council holding its annual meetings alternately in this and one or more adjoining states, may hold its annual meetings for the election of officers and the transaction of business in any adjoining state to this, at such place therein as the said synod, conference or council shall hold its annual meeting; and the elections so held and business so transacted shall be as legal and binding as if held and transacted at the place of business of the corporation in this state.

Sec. 5. In case an election of trustees, directors or managers shall not be made on the day designated by the by-laws, said society for that cause shall not be dissolved, but such election may take place on any other day directed by such by-laws.

Sec. 6. The provisions of this chapter shall not extend or apply to any association or individual who shall, in the certificate filed with the recorder, use or specify a name or style the same as that of any previously existing incorporated society in the county.

Sec. 7. Any corporation formed under this chapter shall be capable of taking, holding or receiving property by virtue of any devise or bequest contained in any last will or testament of any person whatsoever; but no person leaving a wife, child or parent shall devise or bequeath to such institution or incorporation more than one-fourth of his estate after the payment of his debts, and such devise or bequest shall be valid only to the extent of such one-fourth.

Sec. 8. The trustees, directors or stockholders of any existing benevolent, charitable, scientific, missionary or religious corporation may, by conforming to the requirements of section one of this chapter, reincorporate themselves, or continue their existing corporate powers, and all the property and effects of such existing corporation shall vest in and belong to the corporation so reincorporated or continued.

Sec. 9. Any corporation other than those for pecuniary profit may change the corporate name thereof, or amend the articles of incorporation or the original certificate thereto, by a vote of the majority of the members or stockholders of the said corporation in such manner as may be provided by the articles of incorporation thereof.

Sec. 10. In case of the body corporate consisting of the trustees, directors or managers of any benevolent, charitable, literary, scientific, religious or missionary institution under the patronage of any synod, conference, association or other ecclesiastical body in this state, or two or more of them, said amendment or change may originate with either of the said trustees, directors or managers, or with either of the said patronizing bodies; but such change or amendment shall not be made without the vote of a majority of each of said trustees, directors or managers, and of each of the said patronizing bodies, legally expressed and certified thereto by the secretary, clerk or recording officer of such board of trustees, directors or managers and of each of the patronizing bodies.

Sec. 11. The change or amendment of the articles of incorporation shall be recorded by the recorder of deeds as the original articles of incorporation are required to be, and the recorder shall make upon the margin of such record a reference to the book and page of the record of such original articles of incorporation; and from and after the date of such act of recording, such change or amendment shall be in full force and effect as the original articles of incorporation so amended.

Sec. 12. The corporation by its new name, or with such amended articles of incorporation or certificate, shall be entitled to all the rights, powers, immunities and franchises that it possessed before such change or amendment, and shall be liable upon all contracts, obligations, liabilities entered into, incurred or binding on such corporation by or under the old name or articles of incorporation, to the same extent and manner as though no such change or amendment had been made.

CHAPTER X.

IOWA STATUTES OF RELIGIOUS ASSEMBLIES.

Section 1. If any person willfully disturb or disquiet any assembly of persons met for religious worship, by profane discourse or rude and indecent behavior, or by making a noise either within the place of worship or so near as to disturb the order and solemnity of the assembly, he shall be punished by imprisonment in the county jail not more than thirty days, or by fine not exceeding one hundred dollars. If any person, or persons, unlawfully or willfully disturb or interrupt any school, school meeting, teachers' institute, lyceum, literary society, or any other lawful assembly of persons being in the peace of the state, such person or persons shall be deemed guilty of a misdemeanor, and on conviction thereof shall be punished by fine not exceeding one hundred dollars, or by imprisonment in the county jail not exceeding thirty days.

Sec. 2. If any person within one mile from the place where any religious society is collected together for religious worship, in any field or woodland, expose to sale or gift any spirituous or other liquors, or any article of merchandise, or any provisions, or other articles of traffic, he shall be punished by imprisonment in the county jail not more than thirty days, or by fine not exceeding one hundred dollars.

Sec. 3. The preceding section does not apply to tavern or grocery keepers exercising their calling or business in the places mentioned in their licenses, if they have such; nor to any distillers or manufacturers, or others in the prosecution of their ordinary calling or business, so as to prevent them from vending or exposing to sale the articles above prohibited at their place of residence, nor to any person who has a written permit from the person having the charge of such religious society, to sell any of such prohibited articles, on complying with the regulations of such religious assembly and with the laws of the state.

Sec. 4. If any person be found on the first day of the week, commonly called Sabbath, engaged in any riot, fighting or offering to fight, or hunting, shooting, carrying firearms, fishing, horse-racing, dancing, or in any manner disturbing any worshiping assembly or private family, or in buying or selling property of any kind, or in any labor, the work of necessity and charity only excepted, every person so offending shall, on conviction, be fined in a sum not more than five dollars nor less than one dollar, to be recovered before any justice of the peace in the county where such offense is committed, and shall be committed to the jail of said county until the said fine, together with the costs of prosecution, shall be paid; but nothing herein contained shall be construed to extend to those who conscientiously observe the seventh day of the week as the Sabbath, or to prevent persons traveling or families emigrating from pursuing their journey, or keepers of toll bridges, toll gates and ferry-men from attending the same.

Sec. 5. No practicing attorney, counselor, physician, surgeon, minister of the gospel, or priest of any denomination, shall be allowed, in giving testimony, to disclose any confidential communication properly intrusted to him in his professional capacity and necessary and proper to enable him to discharge the functions of his office according to the usual course of practice or discipline. Such prohibition shall not apply to cases where the party in whose favor the same are made waives the rights conferred.

CHAPTER XI.

MICHIGAN STATUTES OF MARRIAGE.

Section 1. Every male who shall have attained the full age of eighteen years, and every female who shall have attained the full age of sixteen years, shall be capable in law of contracting marriage if otherwise competent.

Sec. 2. Marriage, so far as its validity in law is concerned, is a civil contract, to which the consent of parties capable in law of contracting is essential.

Sec. 3. No man shall marry his mother, grandmother, daughter, granddaughter, stepmother, grandfather's wife, son's wife, grandson's wife, wife's mother, wife's grandmother, wife's daughter, wife's granddaughter, nor his sister, brother's daughter, sister's daughter, father's sister, or mother's sister.

Sec. 4. No woman shall marry her father, grandfather, son, grandson, stepfather, grandmother's husband, daughter's husband, granddaughter's husband, husband's father, husband's grandfather, husband's son, husband's grandson, nor her brother, brother's son, sister's son, father's brother, or mother's brother.

Sec. 5. No marriage shall be contracted whilst either of the parties has a former wife or husband living, unless the marriage with such former wife or husband shall have been dissolved.

Sec. 6. No white person shall intermarry with a negro, and no insane person or idiot shall be capable of contracting marriage.

NOTE.—The question whether either of the parties presenting themselves for marriage come within the term "negro," insane person or idiot, within the meaning of the foregoing section, must be determined by the officiating minister, or magistrate, from the preliminary examination, and his own observation, exercising his best judgment. Occasionally a very nice question has been presented to the courts, respecting the meaning of the words "negro," "mulatto," "persons of color," and "white persons." In one case in the State of Maine, Shipley (C. J.) observed: There is a difference of opinion respecting the proportion of African blood which will prevent the person possessing it from being regarded as white. Some courts appear to have held that a person should be so regarded when his white blood predominated both in proportion and in appearance. Those least disposed to consider persons to be white who have any proportion of African blood have admitted that persons possessing only one-eighth part of such blood should be regarded as white. (Bailey *vs.* Fiske, 34 Maine R. 77.)

Sec. 7. Marriages may be solemnized by any justice of the peace in the county in which he is chosen, and they may be solemnized throughout the state by any minister of the gospel, who has been ordained according to the usages of his denomination, and who resides in this state, and continues to be a preacher of the gospel.

Sec. 8. All justices of the peace and ministers of the gospel are hereby authorized and required, before solemnizing any marriage, to examine at least one of the parties on oath, which oath they are hereby authorized to administer as to the legality of such intended marriage.

NOTE.—A neglect to examine one of the parties on oath, according to this section, might subject the officiating officer to the penalty provided in section ten, and simply swearing one of the parties, and asking him or her whether they know of any legal impediment to the marriage, is not enough. The statute requires that he shall *examine* at least one of the parties on oath; when that is done, if the party makes a false statement, the officer is not responsible, provided he has reason to believe such statement to be true, and is satisfied that it is true. But if it plainly appears that there is a legal impediment to such marriage, and he performs the ceremony, he acts willfully, and would be liable to the penalty. No magistrate or minister is obliged to perform the marriage ceremony in any given case; he can decline if he chooses. The following is a proper form of oath to be administered to the party holding up the right hand, or by any other form to him most binding that he may choose:

You do solemnly swear (*or affirm, if the party prefer it*) that you will true answers make to such questions as shall be put to you touching the legality of your intended marriage with Miss E R: So help you God.

Of course any questions may be put after this oath has been administered that may be pertinent or proper, but the following are suggested in order to bring out the facts to be embraced in the record and the certificate required by sections fifteen and sixteen (*post*) of this chapter. It would be a great convenience, and secure correctness, if blanks were provided with the interrogatories printed.

What is your name?
What is your age?
What is your occupation?
What is your place of residence?
Where were you born?
What is the name of this woman?
What is her age?
What is her place of residence?
Where was she born?
Have either of you ever been married?
If so, have either of you a husband or wife living?
If a widow, what was her maiden name?
Are you related to each other by consanguinity or affinity?
If so, what is the relation?
Do you know of any legal impediment to your intended marriage with this woman?

Sec. 9. In the solemnization of marriage no particular form shall be required, except that the parties shall solemnly declare in the presence of the magistrate or minister, and the attending witnesses, that they take each other as husband and wife; and in every case there shall be at least two witnesses besides the minister or magistrate present at the ceremony.

NOTE.—For marriage ceremony see *ante*, pages 26 and 27.

Sec. 10. If any justice of the peace or minister of the gospel shall join any persons in marriage contrary to the provisions of this chapter, he shall forfeit for every such offense a sum not exceeding five hundred dollars.

Sec. 11. If any person shall undertake to join others in marriage knowing that he is not lawfully authorized so to do, or knowing of any legal impediment to the proposed marriage, he shall be deemed guilty of a misdemeanor, and upon conviction thereof shall be punished by imprisonment in the county jail not more than one year, or by a fine not less than fifty nor more than five hundred dollars, or by both; such fine and imprisonment in the discretion of the court.

Sec. 12. No marriage solemnized before any person professing to be a justice of the peace or a minister of the gospel shall be deemed or adjudged to be void, nor shall the validity thereof be in any way affected on account of any want of jurisdiction or authority in such supposed justice or minister, provided the marriage be consummated with the full belief on the part of the persons so married, or either of them, that they have been lawfully joined in marriage.

Sec. 13. The preceding provisions of this chapter, so far as they relate to the manner of solemnizing marriages, shall not affect marriages among the people called Friends or Quakers, nor marriages among people of any other particular denomination having as such any particular mode of solemnizing marriages; but such marriages may be solemnized in the manner heretofore used and practiced in their respective societies or denominations.

Sec. 14. The original certificates and records of marriage made by the minister or justice, as prescribed in this chapter, and the record thereof made by the county clerk, or a copy of such record duly certified by such clerk, shall be received in all courts and places as presumptive evidence of the fact of such marriage.

Sec. 15. Every justice of the peace, minister of the gospel, and all other persons authorized by law to solemnize marriages in this state, shall make a record of each marriage so solemnized by him, and every clerk or keeper of the records of the meetings in which any marriages among the Friends or Quakers shall be solemnized, shall make a record of such marriage, together with all the facts relating to the same, as required by the sixteenth section of this act; and such justice, minister of the gospel, clerk or other person shall, at the time such marriage is solemnized, deliver on demand, to either of the parties so joined in marriage as aforesaid, a certificate of such marriage, containing all the facts in relation thereto required by said sixteenth section of this act, and shall, within ninety days thereafter, deliver to the clerk of the county in which such marriage took place a certified copy of such record, and at the same time pay to the clerk twenty-five cents for recording the same.

Sec. 16. The record of marriages shall state, in separate columns, the date and place of marriage, the christian and surname of the bridegroom and bride, and the maiden name of the bride, if a widow; the color, age and place of birth of each; the residence of each at the time of marriage; the occupation of the bridegroom, and the name and official station of the person by or before whom they were married; the names and residences of at least two witnesses present at such marriage, and the date when such record was made.

FORM OF RECORD.

Record of marriage made on the —— day of ——, 18—.

Date of marriage,
Place of marriage,
Christian and surname of bridegroom,
Age of bridegroom,
Occupation of bridegroom,
Residence of bridegroom,
Birthplace of bridegroom,
Christian and surname of bride,
Maiden name, if a widow, of bride,
Age of bride,
Residence of bride,
Birthplace of bride,
Color of parties (white or colored),

Witnesses: —— ——, of ——, and —— ——, of ——.

Name of person by whom married,

Official station of such person,

Having obtained the above facts by the oath of said —— ——.

NOTE.—CERTIFICATE TO COPY OF ABOVE DELIVERED TO CLERK.

COUNTY OF ——, CITY (*or town*) OF ——.

I certify that the foregoing is a true copy of a record of marriage solemnized by me on the —— day of ——, 18—, and the whole thereof now in my possession.

Witness my hand this —— day of ——, 18—.

—— ——,
Rector (*or Pastor*) of —— Church.

FORM OF MARRIAGE CERTIFICATE.

STATE OF MICHIGAN, } ss.
COUNTY OF ——, }

This is to certify that on the —— day of ——, 18— (*at the residence of* —— ——, *or at* —— *Church*), in the city (*or town*) of ——, State of Michigan, A B, of the age of —— years, by occupation a ——, a resident of ——, who was born at ——, and Miss S P (*if a widow, whose maiden name was* ——), of the age of —— years, a resident of ——, who was born at ——, were with their mutual consent joined in holy matrimony by me (*both white or colored*) in the presence of G H, of ——, and O P, of ——, attending witnesses, a record of which I have this day made according to law.

Given under my hand, at ——, this —— day of ——, 18—.

—— ——,
Rector (*or Pastor*) of —— Church.

Sec. 17. Every justice of the peace, minister of the gospel, and all other persons authorized by the laws of this state to solemnize marriage, and clerks or keepers of records of the meetings in which any marriage among the Friends or Quakers shall be solemnized, who shall neglect or refuse to make a record of such marriage, or to deliver to the county clerk of the county in which the marriage took place a certified copy of such record, or who shall refuse, on demand, to deliver to the parties to such marriage the certificate thereof, as required by section fifteen of this act, or who shall willfully make a false or fictitious entry in his record of marriages, or in the certified copy of such record delivered to the county clerk, or in the certificate of marriage delivered to the parties thereto, shall be deemed guilty of a misdemeanor, and upon conviction thereof shall be punished by a fine not exceeding one hundred dollars, and in default of paying the same shall be imprisoned in the county jail of the county in which such conviction shall be had until said fine be paid, but not to exceed the period of ninety days.

CHAPTER XII.

MICHIGAN STATUTES OF RELIGIOUS SOCIETIES.

Section 1. It shall be lawful for any number of persons of full age, not less than five, who may be desirous of forming themselves into a church congregation or religious society, and who shall sign articles of association for that purpose, to assemble together, at such place as they may select, and by a plurality of votes by ballot, elect any number of discreet persons, being laymen, not less than three nor more than nine in number, as trustees, to take charge of the property belonging to, and transact all the affairs relative to the temporalities of such church congregation or religious society. At any time after such society shall have become duly organized, it shall be lawful for any such church congregation or religious society, at a meeting thereof called in accordance with the provisions of this act, by a vote of two-thirds of the members of such society entitled to vote, present at any such meeting, to amend its articles of association in any manner not inconsistent with the provisions of this act, and such amendments shall become operative on filing a copy of the same certified by the moderator, chairman or president, and clerk of such meeting, with the clerk of the county where such society is organized.

Sec. 2. It shall be lawful for any such church congregation or religious society to choose their minister, priest, curate, rector, parson, or officiating clergyman, for the time being, to be the president of said corporation and of their meetings, by a vote as aforesaid; and at the first election provided for in this act, every person who shall have signed the articles, and at any subsequent election any person of full age who has for six months been a stated worshiper with, or a contributor regularly for one year previous to the support of such church congregation or society shall be entitled to vote.

Sec. 3. The minister, priest, rector, curate, parson, or officiating clergyman of such congregation or society, or if none of them be present, one of the elders or deacons, church-wardens or vestrymen thereof, and for want of such officers any other person being a member or stated hearer in such church congregation or society, shall publicly notify said congregation of the time when and the place where any election shall be held, at least fifteen days before the day of such election, and such notification shall be given for two successive Sabbaths on which such church congregation or society shall statedly meet fo- public worship next preceding the election.

Sec. 4. Any two of the elders, deacons, church-wardens or vestrymen of such church congregation or society, or if such officers shall not be present, then any two voters present, to be nominated by a majority of the voters, shall be inspectors of such election, receive the votes, and determine the qualifications of voters, and they shall immediately after the election certify, under their hands and seals, the names of persons elected to serve as trustees or vestrymen; in which certificate the name by which the said trustees or vestrymen and their successors in office shall forever thereafter be known and called shall be particularly mentioned and specified, and such trustees may in said certificate be denominated vestrymen, or church-wardens and vestrymen, executive committee, or any other name stated in the certificate: *Provided always*, that they shall have all the power specified in this act, and be elected in the manner provided for in this act.

Sec. 5. Such certificate shall be acknowledged by the person making the same, or proved by a subscribing witness thereto, before some officer authorized to take acknowledgments of deeds; and said certificate, with the certificate of acknowledgment or proof thereof, and the articles of association, shall be recorded by the clerk of the county within which the church or place of worship of such congregation shall be situate, in a book to be by him provided for that purpose, who shall be entitled to ten cents for each folio for recording the same; and thereafter such trustees and their successors shall be a body corporate by the name expressed in such certificate.

NOTE.—The following forms may be used under the previous sections:

ARTICLES OF ASSOCIATION.

Know all men by these presents, That we, L M, N O, P Q, R S and T U (*not less than five*), being of full age and desirous of forming ourselves into a church congregation (*or religious society*), do sign these articles of association by which we have agreed, and hereby do agree, to become incorporated such religious society, etc. (*as the case may be*), in pursuance of the law of this state, by the name and style of (*here insert corporate name*), of the (*town, city or village*); and we do hereby agree that all persons who may hereafter become associated with us in this organization shall be entitled to equal privileges and rights in the grant and franchises hereby secured in and by virtue of the statute in such case made and provided.

In witness whereof we have hereunto set our hands and seals this —— day of ——, 18—.

(Signed) L M, [SEAL]
N O, (etc.) [SEAL]

CERTIFICATE OF ELECTION OF OFFICERS.

The undersigned, two of the (*elders, or deacons, or church-wardens, or vestrymen*) of the (*name of church or organization, and if such officers or none of them be present, then any two voters present*), nominated by a majority of votes, inspectors, do hereby certify that on the —— day of ——, 18—, at —— o'clock P.M., at a meeting called and held at ——, in the town of ——, county of ——, and State of Michigan, pursuant to a notice duly given for the purpose of incorporating themselves, did then and there elect by a majority vote of the persons who signed the articles of association, A B, C D and E F (*not less than three nor more than nine*), as trustees of the said church corporation, and the said persons did then and there determine by a like majority of votes that the said trustees or vestrymen and their successors should forever thereafter be known and called by the name of (*give name of church*).

Witness our hands and seals this —— day of ——, 18—.

(Signed) A B, [SEAL]
C D, (etc.) [SEAL]

NOTE.—For form of acknowledgment see *post*, page 125.

Sec. 6. Such trustees may have a common seal and may alter the same at pleasure, and they may take into their possession and custody all the temporalities of such church congregation or society, whether the same shall consist of real or personal estate, and whether the same may have been given, granted or devised, directly or indirectly, to such church congregation or society, or to any other person or persons for their use.

Sec. 7. Such trustees may, also, in their corporate name, sue and be sued in all courts and places, and they may recover and hold all the debts, demands, rights and privileges, all churches, buildings, burying-places, and all the estate and appurtenances belonging to such church congregation or society in whatsoever manner the same may have been acquired, or in whose hands soever the same may be held, as fully and amply as if the right and title thereto had been originally vested in said trustees; and they may hold moneys and personal estate raised or acquired for the purpose of erecting churches, or houses of residence for their minister or priest, or for the purchase of burial ground, for a period not exceeding one year before investment thereof, and not exceeding the value or amount of twenty thousand dollars; and they may hold for a period not exceeding three years, any land which may be lawfully conveyed to them, not exceeding five thousand dollars in value, to be sold for the purpose of raising a fund for erecting, repairing or improving a church, or churches, or other building aforesaid, or for the purchase or improvement of any cemetery or burial-ground. But all such lands shall revert to the donor or grantor, his or her heirs or assigns, if not disposed of within the time aforesaid.

Sec. 8. The said trustees or wardens and vestrymen shall also have authority, under the direction of the society, to sell and convey, mortgage or lease any real estate belonging to such society or held by them as such trustees or wardens and vestrymen, and to erect churches and meeting houses, and dwelling houses for their ministers or priests, and other buildings for the direct and legitimate use of their church congregation or society, and to alter and repair the same, but for no secular purpose: *Provided*, that no such sale or conveyance shall be made in any case where it would be inconsistent with the express terms or plain intent of the grant, donation, conveyance or devise by which the same was conveyed or devised to or for the use of such church congregation or society, nor unless the vote or assent of at least two thirds of those present and entitled to vote at any meeting of the society duly and specially called for that purpose shall be obtained therefor.

Sec. 9. They shall also have authority to make rules and orders for managing the temporal affairs of such church congregation or society, and to dispose of all moneys belonging thereto, and to order and regulate the renting of pews or slips in their meeting houses and churches, and the perquisites for the breaking of the ground and burial of the dead in the cemetery or church-yard, and in the said churches or meeting houses.

Sec. 10. They may appoint a clerk and a treasurer of their board, and a collector to collect their rents and revenues, and may regulate the fees to be allowed such clerk, treasurer and collector, and may remove them and appoint others in their stead at pleasure; and such clerk shall enter all rules and orders made by such trustees, and payments ordered by them, in a book to be procured by them for that purpose.

Sec. 11. Any two of the trustees may at any time call a meeting of the trustees, and a majority of them, being lawfully convened, shall be competent to do and perform all matters and things which such trustees are authorized to do and perform; and said trustees may elect the minister, priest, curate, rector, parson or officiating clergyman of said society for the time being, to preside at such meetings, who shall have no vote except in case of a tie of the board, when he shall have a casting vote.

Sec. 12. The said trustees shall hold their offices for three years; and immediately after their first election as hereinbefore provided, the said trustees shall be divided by lot into three classes, numbered one, two and three; and the seats of the first class shall be vacated at the end of the first year, of the second class at the end of the second year, and of the third class at the end of the third year, to the end that, as near as may be, one third part of the whole number of the trustees may be annually chosen: *Provided, however*, that any persons entering into articles of association as aforesaid, may provide in said articles for the election of the whole board of trustees once in each year, at such time as they may appoint, in the manner above prescribed, and said whole number may be elected in conformity to such provisions.

Sec. 13. It shall be the duty of the clerk of said trustees, at least one month before the expiration of the office of any of said trustees, to notify the same in writing to the minister, priest, curate, rector, parson or officiating clergyman, or in case of his death or absence, to the elders or church-wardens, or if there be no elders or church-wardens, then to the deacons or vestrymen of any such church congregation or society, specifying in such notice the names of the trustees whose office will expire; and the minister, priest, curate, rector, parson or other officer receiving such notice shall, in manner aforesaid, notify the members of such church congregation or society of such vacancies, and appoint the time and place for the election to supply the same.

Sec. 14. Such election shall be held at least six days before vacancies shall occur as aforesaid; and all such subsequent elections shall be held and conducted by the like persons, and in the same manner, as hereinbefore provided for the first election; and in case any vacancy shall occur by the death of a trustee, his refusal to act, or removal from the society before his term of office expires, or otherwise, notice thereof shall be given as aforesaid, and an election shall be held and another trustee chosen in his stead for the remainder of his term.

Sec. 15. No person belonging to any such church congregation or society incorporated under the provisions of this act, shall be entitled to vote at any election after the first until he shall have been an attendant on public worship in such church congregation or society at least six months next before such election, and shall have contributed to the support of such church congregation or society according to the usages and customs thereof.

Sec. 16. The clerk of the trustees shall keep a register of the names of all such persons as shall desire to become stated hearers in the said church congregation or society, and shall therein note the time when such request was made; and the said clerk shall attend all subsequent elections in order to test the qualifications of such voters in case they shall be questioned.

Sec. 17. Nothing in this act contained shall be construed to give such trustees the power to fix or ascertain the salary or compensation to be paid any minister, priest, curate, rector or parson, but the same shall be ascertained and fixed by a majority of such society entitled to vote at the election of trustees.

Sec. 18. It shall be lawful for the circuit court for the county in which any such religious corporation shall have been constituted, on the application of such corporation, if such court shall deem it proper, to make an order for the sale of any real estate belonging to such corporation, and to direct the application of the moneys arising therefrom to such uses as the said corporation, with the approbation of said court, shall conceive to be for the interest of such corporation: *Provided*, that no such sale shall be authorized by the court in any case where it would be inconsistent with the express terms or plain intent of the grant, donation, conveyance or devise by which the same was conveyed or devised to or for the use of such church congregation or society prior to the passage of this act.

Sec. 19. At least thirty days' previous notice of any such application to the circuit court shall be given by publishing the same in some newspaper published in the county, if one be there published; if not, by posting up notices in three or more public places in such county.

Sec. 20. All lands, tenements, and hereditaments that have been or may hereafter be lawfully conveyed by devise, gift, grant, purchase or otherwise, to any persons as trustees, in trust for the use of any church congregation or religious society, organized, or which may hereafter be organized within this state, either for a meeting-house, burial-ground, or for the residence of a preacher or priest, shall vest and descend, with the improvements, in perpetual succession to, and shall be held by the trustees provided for in this act, in trust for such church congregation or society.

Sec. 21. No bishop, vicar, rector, parson, curate, priest, deacon or other officer of any church, religious body, order, society or association; no superior or other officer or member, male or female, of any religious order, ecclesiastical or lay, nor of any ecclesiastical, educational or charitable institution or establishment, shall in consequence of such office or membership, or in the character or capacity of such officer or member, have, possess or exercise any power, capacity or franchise of a corporation sole, so far as relates to the taking, holding, managing, selling or transmitting property; and every gift, grant, devise, bequest, conveyance, or lease of any real estate or any interest therein, or any use or benefit to arise therefrom, or of money or of other property to be invested therein or to arise therefrom, hereafter made or attempted to be made, by deed, will or otherwise, to any such officer or member by his or her name of office or membership, or in the character of such officer or member, shall be utterly void to all intents and purposes, and no corporation for religious, ecclesiastical, educational or charitable purposes, shall be recognized as existing by the common law, the canon law, or by prescription, or in any other manner except by express statute of this state: *Provided*, that this section shall in no way invalidate any right of property or right of action heretofore vested; *and provided further*, that this section is not intended as any implication or admission of any previous corporate capacity incident to such official character or membership as herein above mentioned.

Sec. 22. Neither the canon law nor the decrees, nor any decree or order of any ecclesiastical council or body, nor any custom or usage founded thereon, nor any custom or usage of any church congregation or religious society or religious order shall hereafter be recognized or enforced in this state so far as such law, usage or custom shall relate to the acquisition, the tenure, or the control or disposition of any real estate or any interest therein, or any use or trust connected or to be connected therewith: *Provided nevertheless*, that this section shall not in any manner impair or invalidate any grant, devise or other conveyance heretofore made, nor shall this section be construed as a recognition of the prior legality or obligation of such law, usage or custom in this state.

Sec. 23. No grant, conveyance, devise or lease of any real estate, dedicated or appropriated to the purposes of religious worship, or for any religious or ecclesiastical purposes, or appearing to be intended to be managed or controlled by any congregation or society, or any officer or officers thereof, in his or their official capacity, shall hereafter vest any right, title or interest in any person or persons to whom such grant, conveyance, devise or lease may be made, unless the same shall be made to a corporation organized under some statute of this state, or of the late Territory of Michigan, or under the provisions of this act or some act hereafter passed, amending or altering the same.

Sec. 24. Every church congregation or religious society heretofore incorporated in pursuance of any statute of this state, or of the late Territory of Michigan, and not since dissolved, shall be and is hereby established and confirmed, subject, nevertheless, to the provisions of this act, so far as they may be constitutionally subjected thereto without impairing rights heretofore legally vested. And all vacancies which may hereafter occur in the office of trustee of any church or religious society, heretofore incorporated under any statute of this state, or of the late Territory of Michigan, shall be filled by an election as provided for the filling of vacancies in such office under this act; and in case of the dissolution of any such corporation, or of any corporation hereafter to be formed in pursuance of the provisions of this act, for any cause whatever, the same may be incorporated under the provisions of this act at any time within six years after such dissolution, and thereupon all the estate, real and personal, formerly belonging to the same, and not lawfully disposed of, shall vest in such corporation, as if there had been no dissolution.

Sec. 25. The provisions of this chapter shall apply to all churches, religious congregations, religious societies, religious and ecclesiastical orders, and every association of persons for religious purposes.

NOTE.—The following acts relating to particular religious societies may be found by referring to the Compiled Laws of 1871, viz.: An act for the organization of Protestant Episcopal churches, page 1043; An act to provide for the appointment of trustees in certain cases, page 1045; An act to enable certain Protestant Episcopal churches to reorganize, page 1046; An act to provide for the incorporation of Presbyterian churches, page 1047; An act to provide for the incorporation of Reformed Protestant Dutch churches, page 1049; An act to provide for the incorporation of churches of Christ, page 1051; An act to provide for the union and consolidation of churches of Christ, page 1053; An act to authorize the organization of young men's Christian associations, page 1055; An act to authorize the Roman Catholic bishops of Michigan to hold property in trust for the use of the church, page 1056; An act to provide for the incorporation of St. Jean Baptiste societies, page 1057; An act to provide for the incorporation of associations, conventions, conferences, or religious bodies for literary, religious or other benevolent purposes, page 1059; An act to amend an act for the incorporation of associations, conventions, religious bodies, etc., page 2, laws of 1875; An act to provide for the exercise by religious societies of corporate powers for certain purposes, page 26, laws 1875.

CHAPTER XIII.

MICHIGAN STATUTES OF RELIGIOUS ASSEMBLIES.

Section I. Every person who, on the first day of the week or at any other time, shall willfully interrupt or disturb any assembly of people met for the worship of God, within the place of such meeting or out of it, shall, on conviction thereof before any justice of the peace, be punished by imprisonment in the county jail not more than thirty days, or by a fine not exceeding fifty dollars.

Sec. 2. No person shall willfully disturb, interrupt or disquiet any assembly of people met for religious worship by profane discourse, by rude and indecent behavior, or by making a noise, either within the place of worship or so near it as to disturb the order and solemnity of the meeting; nor shall any person, within two miles of the place where any religious society shall be actually assembled for religious worship, expose to sale or gift any ardent or distilled liquors, wine, beer, cider, fruit, or any other article of food or merchandise, or keep open any huckster-shop in any other place, inn, stand or grocery than such as shall be or have been duly licensed, or in which such person shall have usually carried on such business; nor shall any person, within the distance aforesaid, exhibit any shows or plays unless the same shall have been duly licensed by the proper authority; nor shall any person within the distance aforesaid promote, aid or be engaged in any racing of any animals, or in any gaming of any description; nor shall any person obstruct the free passage of any highway to any place of public worship within the distance aforesaid.

Sec. 3. Whoever shall violate either of the provisions of the foregoing section may be convicted summarily before any justice of the peace of the county, or any mayor, recorder, alderman or other magistrate of any city or township where the offense shall be committed, and on such conviction shall forfeit a sum not exceeding twenty-five dollars, for the benefit of the township libraries in the township in which such conviction is had.

Sec. 4. It shall be the duty of all sheriffs and their deputies, coroners, marshals, constables and other peace officers, all presiding elders and ministers of the gospel, deacons, stewards and official members of any church or religious society who may be present at the meeting of any assembly for religious worship, which shall be interrupted or disturbed in the manner herein prohibited, on sight to apprehend the offender and take him before some justice of the peace or other magistrate authorized to convict as aforesaid, to be proceeded against according to law.

CONSTITUTIONAL PROVISIONS.

Sec. 5. The legislature shall pass no law to prevent any person from worshiping Almighty God according to the dictates of his own conscience, or to compel any person to attend, erect or support any place of religious worship, or to pay tithes, taxes or other rates for the support of any minister of the gospel or teacher of religion.

Sec. 6. No money shall be appropriated or drawn from the treasury for the benefit of any religious sect or society, theological or religious seminary, nor shall property belonging to the state be appropriated for any such purposes.

Sec. 7. The legislature shall not diminish or enlarge the civil or political rights, privileges and capacities of any person on account of his opinion or belief concerning matters of religion.

NOTE.—The following property is exempt from taxation. See Sec. 5 Compiled Laws of 1871.

Sec. 8. All the houses of public worship, with the pews or slips and furniture therein, also the land on which such houses of worship may stand, so far as occupied by such houses of worship and for no other purposes, and rights of burial and tombs while in use as repositories of the dead, and also any parsonage owned and occupied as such by any religious society incorporated under the laws of this state.

Sec. 9. All property held by any religious society as a ministerial fund shall be assessed to the treasurer of such society, and if such property consists of real estate it shall be taxed in the township where such property lies; if it consists of personal property it shall be taxed in the township where such society usually holds its meetings.

CHAPTER XIV.

MINNESOTA STATUTES OF MARRIAGE.

Section 1. *Marriage a civil contract.*—Marriage, so, far as its validity in law is concerned, is a civil contract, to which the consent of the parties, capable in law of contracting, is essential.

Sec. 2. *Who is capable of contracting marriage.*—Every male person who has attained the full age of eighteen years, and every female who has attained the full age of fifteen years, is capable in law of contracting marriage, if otherwise competent.

Sec. 3. *Persons prohibited from marrying.*—No marriage shall be contracted while either of the parties has a husband or a wife living, nor between parties who are nearer of kin than first cousins, computing by the rules of the civil law, whether the half or the whole blood.

Sec. 4. *Marriages, by whom solemnized.*—Marriages may be solemnized by any justice of the peace in the county in which he is elected; and throughout the state by any judge of a court of record, or any ordained minister of the gospel in regular communion with any religious society.

Sec. 5. *Ministers shall file copy of credentials with*

clerk of court.—Ministers of the gospel, before they are authorized to perform the marriage rite, shall file a copy of their credentials of ordination with the clerk of the district court of some county in this state, who shall record the same and give a certificate thereof; and the place where such credentials are recorded shall be indorsed upon each certificate of marriage granted by any minister and recorded with the same.

Sec. 6. *One of the parties may be examined on oath.*—All judges, justices of the peace and ministers of the gospel may, before solemnizing any marriage, examine at least one of the parties on oath, which oath they are authorized to administer as to the legality of such intended marriage; and in no case shall such judge, justice or minister solemnize a marriage if he is satisfied that there is any legal impediment thereto.

NOTE.—This section does not make it imperative on the officiating minister to examine at least one of the parties on oath as to the legality of such intended marriage, but it is safe to do so if there is any doubt about the qualifications of either of the parties, as he is strictly forbidden to solemnize a marriage if he is satisfied that there is any legal impediment; and by section thirteen (*post*) he incurs a severe penalty if he knowingly solemnize any marriage contrary to the provisions of this chapter. The only way to thoroughly inform himself is to examine one of the parties on oath, and take his or her answers in writing, and if the answers are false, yet if they show the parties qualified, the clergyman would be exonerated, as he has done his full duty, unless it should be made to appear that he had knowledge aside from the statements of the parties that there was some legal impediment.

No magistrate or minister is obliged to perform the marriage ceremony in any given case; he can decline if he choose.

The following is a proper form of oath to be administered to the party holding up the right hand:

You do solemnly swear (*or affirm, if the party prefers*) that you will true answers make to such questions as shall be put to you touching the legality of your intended marriage with Miss E N: So help you God.

Of course any questions may be put after this oath has been administered that may be pertinent or proper, but the following are suggested in order to bring out the material facts, viz.:

What is your full name?
What is the name of this woman?
Where do you reside?
Where does she reside?
What is your age?
What is her age?
Have either of you ever been married?
If so, have either of you a husband or wife living?
Are you related to each other?
If so, what is the relation?
Do you know of any legal impediment to your marriage with this woman?

The party being under oath, if any of the answers to these questions are false, he can be convicted of perjury and made to suffer the penalty.

Sec. 7. *License to be obtained, when.*—Previous to persons being joined in marriage a license shall be obtained from the clerk of the district court of the county in which the female resides; or, if not a resident of this state, then from the clerk of the district court in the county where the marriage is to take place in this state; but if there shall be no such clerk in the county where such female resides or where the marriage is to be solemnized, then no such license shall be required.

Sec. 8. *Clerk to make inquiries, and to be satisfied that there is no legal impediments.*—The clerk of the district court, as aforesaid, may inquire of the party applying for marriage license as aforesaid, upon oath or affirmation, relative to the legality of such contemplative marriage, and if the clerk shall be satisfied that there is no legal impediment thereto, then he shall grant such marriage license, and shall make a record thereof; and if any persons intending to marry shall be under age, and shall not have had a former wife or husband, the consent of the parents or guardians shall be personally given before the clerk, or certified under the hand of such parent or guardian, attested by two witnesses, one of whom shall appear before said clerk and make oath or affirmation that he saw said parent or guardian subscribe, or heard him or her acknowledge the same; and said clerk is hereby authorized to administer such oath or affirmation, and thereupon issue and sign such license, and affix thereto the seal of the court. The clerk shall be entitled to receive as his fee for administering the oath and granting the license with the seal affixed thereto, recording the certificate of marriage and filing the necessary papers, the sum of two dollars; and if any clerk shall in any other manner issue or sign any marriage license he shall forfeit and pay a sum not exceeding one thousand dollars, to and for the use of the parties aggrieved.

Sec. 9. *No particular form of marriage required.*—In the solemnization of marriage no particular form is required, except that the parties shall declare in the presence of the judge, minister or magistrate and the attending witnesses, that they take each other as husband and wife; and in every case there shall be at least two witnesses present besides the persons performing the ceremony.

NOTE.—For form of ceremony see *ante*, pages 26 and 27.

Sec. 10. *Certificate to be given.*—Whenever a marriage is solemnized, the person solemnizing the same shall give to each of the parties, if requested, a certificate thereof, specifying therein the names and residence of the parties, and of at least two of the witnesses present, and the time and place of such marriage.

CERTIFICATE OF MARRIAGE.

This is to certify that A B, of ——, in the county of ——, and State of ——, and E R, of ——, in the county of ——, and State of ——, were joined in holy matrimony by me at ——, in the State of Minnesota, this —— day of ——, in the year of our Lord one thousand eight hundred and ——, in the presence of T L, of ——, in the county of ——, and State of ——, and W S, of ——, in the county of ——, and State of Minnesota, attending witnesses, the said A B having produced the requisite license and being first examined under oath by me (*if that is the fact*), and no legal impediment being found thereto.

Given under my hand this —— day of ——, 18—.

—— ——

Rector (*or Pastor*) of —— Church.

NOTE.—Indorse upon the back of each certificate of marriage as follows:

My credentials of ordination are recorded in the office of the clerk of the district court of the county of ——, in the State of Minnesota.

—— ——,

Rector (*or Pastor*) of —— Church.

Sec. 11. *Record to be made and certificate delivered to clerk of court—Certificate to be recorded.*—Every person solemnizing a marriage shall make a certificate under his hand, containing the particulars specified in the next preceding section, and shall deliver the same to the clerk of the district court in the same county where the license was issued, and a duplicate with the clerk in the county where the marriage was solemnized, which certificate shall be filed and recorded by said clerk in a book to be kept by him for that purpose; and said clerk shall be entitled to receive the sum of twenty-five cents for recording said duplicate certificate from the person offering the same for record.

NOTE.—The above duplicate certificates may be like that given to the parties; and this part of a clergyman's duty is quite important for the purpose of enabling the proper officers to make a public record of the marriage, but it is a duty often neglected, although the law fixes a penalty to such neglect of not to exceed one hundred dollars fine.

Sec. 12. *Failure to deliver certificate—Penalty.*—Every person solemnizing a marriage, who neglects to make and deliver to the clerk a certificate thereof within the time above specified, shall forfeit a sum not more than one hundred dollars; and every clerk who neglects to record such certificate so delivered shall forfeit the like penalty.

Sec. 13. *Penalty for solemnizing marriage contrary to law, or making false certificate.*—If any person authorized by law to join persons in marriage knowingly solemnizes any marriage contrary to the provisions of this chapter, or willfully makes any false certificate of any marriage or pretended marriage, he shall forfeit for every such offense a sum not exceeding five hundred dollars or may be imprisoned not exceeding one year.

Sec. 14. *Penalty on persons undertaking to join others in marriage when not authorized, etc.*—If any person undertakes to join others in marriage knowing that he is not lawfully authorized to do so, or knowing of any legal impediment in the proposed marriage, he shall be guilty of a misdemeanor, and upon conviction thereof shall be punished by imprisonment not more than one year or by a fine not more than five hundred dollars, or by both such fine and imprisonment, in the discretion of the court.

Sec. 15. *When marriages not void although person officiating was not authorized.*—No marriage solemnized before any person professing to be judge, justice of the peace or minister of the gospel, shall be deemed or adjudged to be void, nor shall the validity thereof be in any way affected, on account of want of jurisdiction or authority in such supposed judge, justice or minister, provided the marriage is consummated with a full belief on the part of the persons so married, or either of them, that they have been lawfully joined in marriage.

Sec. 16. *Marriages among Quakers valid—Duty of clerk—Penalty.*—All marriages solemnized among the people called Friends or Quakers in the form heretofore practiced and in use in their meetings are valid, and not affected by any of the foregoing provisions; and the clerk of the meeting in which such marriage is solemnized shall, within one month after every such marriage, deliver a certificate of the same to the clerk of the district court of the county where such marriage took place, or of the county to which such county is attached for judicial purposes, in a penalty of forfeiting not more than one hundred dollars, which certificate shall be filed and recorded by such clerk under a like penalty; and if such marriage does not take place in such meeting such certificate shall be signed by the parties and at least six witnesses present, and filed and recorded as above provided under a like penalty.

Sec. 17. *Illegitimate children legitimatized by marriage of parents.*—Illegitimate children become legitimatized by the subsequent marriage of their parents with each other, and the issue of marriages declared null in law shall nevertheless be legitimate.

CHAPTER XV.

MINNESOTA STATUTES OF RELIGIOUS ASSEMBLIES.

Section 1. *Disturbing public worship, how punished.*—Whoever on the Lord's day, or at any other time, willfully interrupts or disturbs any assembly of the people met for worship, within the place of said meeting or out of it, shall be punished by fine not exceeding twenty dollars nor less than five dollars, or by imprisonment in the county jail not exceeding thirty days.

Sec. 2. No person shall keep open his shop, warehouse or workhouse, or shall do any manner of labor, business or work, except only works of necessity and charity, or be present at any dancing or any public diversion, show or entertainment, or take part in any sport, game or play on the Lord's day, commonly called Sunday; and every person so offending shall be punished by a fine not exceeding two dollars for each offense.

Sec. 3. No person shall keep any shop, booth, tent, wagon, carriage for the sale of, or shall sell, give or expose to sale any spirituous or intoxicating liquors, goods or merchandise of any kind within two miles of any public assembly, camp or grove meeting convened for the purpose of religious worship; but this shall not be construed to prevent any person from selling merchandise at the shop or store where he usually transacts business; nor from selling liquors in any place where he has received a license therefor before the appointment of such religious meeting; nor to prevent any peddler from selling his goods to any person at the usual place of business or residence of such person.

Sec. 4. Whoever is guilty of a breach of the preceding section, upon conviction thereof before any justice of the peace shall be fined not exceeding thirty dollars or imprisonment in the county jail for any term not exceeding thirty days, or may be sentenced to both said punishments.

Sec. 5. Whoever is guilty of noisy, rude or indecent behavior of exhibiting shows or plays or promoting or engaging in horse-racing or gambling at or near any such religious meeting so as to interrupt or disturb the same, or at any religious meeting of the citizens of this state maliciously cuts or otherwise injures or destroys any harness or tents, or other property belonging to any tent holder or other person, upon conviction thereof before any justice of the peace shall be fined not exceeding fifty dollars, or if the offense is of an aggravated nature he may be held to recognize with sufficient sureties to appear at the district court next to be holden in the same county, and upon conviction before such court he shall be fined in any sum not exceeding one hundred dollars or imprisoned in the county jail not exceeding ninety days, or by both such fine and imprisonment.

Sec. 6. No prosecution for any violation of the provisions of the last three sections shall be sustained unless commenced within sixty days after the commission of such offense.

Sec. 7. For the purposes of the provisions of the second section the Lord's day shall include the time between the midnight preceding and the midnight following the said day.

CONSTITUTION.

Sec. 8. *Freedom of religious belief acknowledged.*—The enumeration of rights in this constitution shall not be construed to deny or impair others retained by and inherent in the people. The right of every man to worship God according to the dictates of his own conscience shall never be infringed, nor shall any man be compelled to attend, erect or support any place of worship or to maintain any religious or ecclesiastical ministry against his consent, nor shall any control of or interference with the rights of conscience be permitted, or any preference be given by law to any religious establishment or mode of worship; but the liberty of conscience hereby secured shall not be so construed as to excuse acts of licentiousness or justify practices inconsistent with the peace or safety of the state, nor shall any money be drawn from the treasury for the benefit of any religious societies or religious or theological seminaries.

CHAPTER XVI.

MINNESOTA STATUTES OF RELIGIOUS CORPORATIONS.

Section 1. *Religious corporations, how organized.*—It shall be lawful for all persons of full age belonging to any church congregation or religious society not already incorporated, to assemble at the church or meeting house, or other place where they statedly attend for divine worship, and by a plurality vote elect any number of discreet persons of their church congregation or society, not less than three nor more than nine in number, as trustees, to take charge of the estate and property belonging thereto, and transact all affairs relative to the temporalities thereof.

Sec. 2. *President shall be chosen — Who may vote.*—Such church congregation or religious society may choose a president of the said corporation and of their meetings, by a vote as aforesaid; and at the election provided for in this chapter, every person of full age who has statedly worshiped with such church congregation or society, and has been formally considered as belonging thereto, is entitled to a vote.

Sec. 3. *Notice of election, how given.*—The minister of such congregation or society, and in case of his death or absence, one of the elders or deacons, church-wardens or vestrymen thereof, and for want of such officers any other person being a member or stated hearer in such church congregation or society, shall publicly notify the congregation of the time when and the place where the said election shall be held, at least fifteen days before the day of election; and such notification shall be given for two successive Sabbaths on which such church congregation or society statedly meet for public worship preceding the election.

Sec. 4. *Election, how conducted.* — Any two of the elders, deacons, church-wardens or vestrymen of such church congregation or society, or if such officers are not present, then any two voters present, to be nominated by a majority of the voters, shall preside at such election, receive the votes and determine the qualification of voters; and they shall, immediately after the election, certify under their hands and seals the names of the persons elected to serve as trustees, in which certificate the name by which the said trustees and their successors in office shall forever thereafter be called and known, shall be particularly mentioned and specified.

FORM OF CERTIFICATE.

To all whom it may concern:

The undersigned, two of the (*elders, deacons, church-wardens, vestrymen or voters*), at a meeting of the members of the church (*or congregation*), of full age, of—— Church (*or Society*) for the election of officers appointed to receive the votes of all qualified voters at such election and canvass the same, do hereby certify that on the —— day of ——, 18—, at —— Church (*or other place of worship of said congregation*), in the town of ——, county of ——, State of Minnesota, held in pursuance of notice to the congregation of said church or society, given at two stated meetings on two successive Sabbaths, being fifteen days previous to such meeting, and at said meeting O P, Q R, and S T (*not to exceed nine*) were duly elected, by a plurality vote, trustees of said church (*or society*), and it was then and there determined, by a like vote, that the name by which said trustees and their successors in office should forever thereafter be called and known be, The Trustees of —— Church, of ——.

Witness our hands and seals this —— day of ——, 18—.

A B. [SEAL]
C D. [SEAL]

Sec. 5. *Certificate to be acknowledged and recorded.*—Such certificate shall be acknowledged by the persons making the same, or proved by a subscribing witness thereto, before some officer authorized to take the acknowledgment of deeds, and recorded, together with the certificate of such acknowledgment, or proof by the register of deeds of the county within which the church or place of worship of such congregation is situated, in a book provided by him for that purpose, who shall be entitled to receive seventy-five cents for such record; and thereafter such trustees and their successors shall be a body corporate by the name expressed in such certificate.

NOTE.—For form of acknowledgment see *post*, page 125.

Sec. 6. *Trustees to have seal—May do what.*—Such trustees may have a common seal, and alter the same at pleasure; they may take into their possession and custody all the temporalities of such church congregation or society, whether the same consists of real or personal estate, and have been given, granted or devised, directly or indirectly, to such church congregation or society, or to any other person for their use.

Sec. 7. *General powers of trustees.*—Such trustees may also, in their corporate name, sue and be sued in all courts and places, and they may recover and hold all the debts, demands, rights and privileges, all churches, buildings, burial-places, and all the estate and appurtenances belonging to such church congregation or society, in whatsoever manner the same may have been acquired, or in whose hands soever the same may be held, as fully and amply as if the right and title thereto had been originally vested in the said trustees; and they may hold other real or personal estate, and demise, lease and improve the same; but the whole of such estate, real and personal, shall not exceed the yearly income of three thousand dollars.

Sec. 8. *May erect and repair churches and parsonages.*—The said trustees have authority to repair and alter their churches and meeting houses, and, under the direction of the society or congregation, erect churches and meeting houses and dwelling houses for their ministers, and other buildings for the use of their church congregation or society.

Sec. 9. *May make by-laws, rent pews, etc.*—They have authority to make rules and orders for managing the temporal affairs of such church congregation or society, and to dispose of all moneys belonging thereto; and to order and regulate the renting of pews or slips in their churches and meeting houses, and the requisites for the breaking of ground in the cemetery or churchyard and in the said churches or meeting houses for burying the dead.

Sec. 10. *May appoint clerk and treasurer.*—They may appoint a clerk and treasurer of their board, and a collector to collect and receive their rents and revenues, and may regulate the fees to be allowed to such clerk, treasurer and collector, and may remove them and appoint others in their stead at pleasure; and such clerk shall enter all rules and orders made by such trustees and payments ordered by them, in a book to be procured by them for that purpose.

Sec. 11. *Meetings, how called and conducted.*—Any two of the trustees may at any time call a meeting of the trustees, and a majority of them being lawfully convened, shall be competent to do and perform all matters and things which such trustees are authorized to do and perform.

Sec. 12. *Trustees to hold office three years.*—The said trustees shall hold their offices for three years, and immediately after their first election as hereinbefore provided, the said trustees shall be divided by lot into three classes, numbered one, two and three; and the seats of the first class shall be vacated at the end of the first year, of the second class at the end of the second year, and of the third class at the end of the third year; and as near as may be one-third part of the whole number of trustees may be annually chosen.

Sec. 13. *Clerk to give notice of expiration of term of office of trustees.*—The clerk of said trustees, at least one month before the expiration of the office of any of the said trustees, shall notify the same in writing to the minister, or in case of his death or absence, to the elders or church-wardens, and if there are no elders or church-wardens, then to the deacons or vestrymen of any such church congregation or society, specifying in such notice the names of the trustees whose office will expire; and the minister or other officers receiving such notice shall, in the manner aforesaid, notify the members of such church congregation or society of such vacancies, and appoint the time and place for the election to supply the same.

Sec. 14. *Election of trustees, how conducted.*—Such election shall be held at least six days before vacancies happen as aforesaid, and all such subsequent elections shall be held and conducted in the same manner as hereinbefore provided for the first election; and in case any vacancy happens by the death of a trustee, his refusal to act, or removal from the society before his term of office expires or otherwise, notice thereof shall be given as aforesaid, and an election shall be held and another trustee chosen in his stead for the remainder of such term.

Sec. 15. *Qualifications of voters.*—No person belonging to any such church congregation or society, incorporated under the provisions of this chapter, is entitled to vote at any election after the first until he has been an attendant on public worship in such church congregation or society at least six months before such election, and contributed to the support of such church congregation or society, according to the usages and customs thereof.

Sec. 16. *Clerk to keep register of stated hearers.*—The clerk of the trustees shall keep a register of the names of all such persons as desire to become stated hearers in said church congregation or society, and shall therein note the time when such request was made, and the said clerk shall attend all subsequent elections in order to test the qualifications of such voters in case they shall be questioned.

Sec. 17. *Salary of ministers.*—Nothing in this title (chapter) contained shall be construed to give such trustees the power to fix or ascertain the salary or compensation to be paid to any minister, but the same shall be ascertained and fixed by a majority of such society entitled to vote at the election of trustees.

Sec. 18. (As amended by acts of March 9, 1876, and February 27, 1872.) *Trustees may sell or incumber real estate — The word society defined.*—It shall be lawful for any religious corporation organized under the provisions of this title, by and through their trustees, to sell and convey, incumber or otherwise dispose of any real estate belonging to such corporation: *Provided, however*, that no such conveyance or incumbrance shall be made by the trustees, except when first authorized to make the same by a resolution of such society, passed at a meeting thereof called for that purpose, notice of the time, place and object of which meeting shall be given for at least four successive Sabbaths on which such society statedly meet for public worship immediately preceding the time specified for such meeting; and proof of the facts of such notice, meetings and resolutions may be made by the affidavits of one such trustee or by any member of such society cognizant of the facts. Such affidavits may be recorded at length in the office of the register of deeds of the county where the premises are situated, and the same and the records thereof aforesaid, or certified copies of such records, shall be presumptive evidence of the facts contained therein: *and provided further*, that by the word "society," as used in this section, shall be understood the religious body, constituted in accordance with its own principles of ecclesiastical polity, which form the basis of the corporation designated in this title "the church society or congregation," and as contradistinguished from such corporation; and no person shall vote at any meeting called as aforesaid to authorize said trustees to sell and convey, incumber or otherwise dispose of any real estate belonging to such corporation, who is not a member of such religious body.

Sec. 19. *Existing societies confirmed—Corporations heretofore dissolved may organize anew within six years after dissolution.*—Every church congregation or religious society heretofore incorporated in pursuance of law, and not since dissolved, is hereby established and confirmed; and in case of the dissolution of any such corporation, or of any corporation hereafter to be formed, in pursuance of the provisions of this title, for any cause whatever, the same may be incorporated under the provisions of this title at any time within six years after such discussion; and thereupon all the estate, real and personal, formerly belonging to the same, and not lawfully disposed of, shall vest in such corporation as if there had been no such dissolution.

Sec. 20. *Descent of land held by trustees.*—All lands, tenements, and hereditaments lawfully conveyed by devise, grant, purchase or otherwise to any persons as trustees in trust for the use of any religious society organized, or which may hereafter be organized within this state, either for a meeting house, burying-ground, or for the residence of a preacher, shall descend with the improvements in perpetual succession to, and shall be held by, such trustees in trust for such society.

Sec. 21. *Minister to give certificate of appointment of trustees, when.*—Whenever by the constitution, rules or usages of any particular church or religious denomination, trustees are required to be appointed by any ministers, presiding elders, or other officer or officers of such church or denomination, such ministers, presiding elders, or other officer or officers, shall give to such trustees a certificate of their appointment under the hand and seal of the person making the same, specifying the name by which such trustees and their successors shall forever thereafter be called and known, which certificate shall be acknowledged and proved and recorded as hereinbefore directed; whereupon such trustees and their successors appointed in the same manner shall be a body corporate by the name expressed in such certificate, with all the rights, powers and privileges of other religious corporations constituted according to the provisions of this title.

CERTIFICATE.

To all to whom these presents shall come: This is to certify that F M, O P, etc., are hereby appointed trustees of —— (*church or society*) for the term of —— years, and that the name by which said trustees and their successors shall forever thereafter be called and known shall be (*here give name in full*).

Witness our (*or my*) hand(*s*) and seal(*s*) this —— day of ——, 18—.

W P, [SEAL]
Minister (*or Pastor*).
R S, [SEAL]
Elder.

NOTE.—See form of acknowledgment, *post*, page 125.

Sec. 22. *When ministers, elders and deacons are trustees they may execute certificate.*—Whenever by the constitution, rules and usages of any particular church or religious denomination the minister or ministers, elders and deacons or other officers elected by any church or congregation, according to such constitution, rules or usages, are thereby constituted the trustees of such church or congregation, such minister or ministers, elders and deacons, or other officers, may assemble together and execute, under their hands and seals, a certificate, stating therein the name by which they and their successors in office shall forever thereafter be called and known, which certificate shall be acknowledged or proved and recorded as hereinbefore directed; whereupon such persons and their successors in office shall be a body corporate by the name expressed in such certificate, with all the rights, powers and privileges of other religious corporations constituted according to the provisions of this title.

CERTIFICATE.

To all whom it may concern: This is to certify that the undersigned ——, *minister or* ——, *and* —— (*elders or deacons, as the case may be*), constituted trustees of the (*name of church or society*), assembled together at the —— church (*or house of S T*), in the city of ——, on the —— day of —— 18—, and then and there determined, by a plurality of votes, that the name by which such trustees and their successors in office should forever thereafter be called and known, should be (*here give name in full*).

Witness our hands and seals this —— day of ——, 18—.

A B. [SEAL]
C D. [SEAL]
E F. [SEAL]

NOTE.—See form of acknowledgment, *post*, page 125.

Sec. 23. *Members of the Protestant Episcopal church may elect church-wardens— Vacancies, how filled.*—It shall be lawful for the male persons, of full age, of any church or congregation in communion with the Protestant Episcopal church in this state, who have belonged to such church or congregation for the last three months preceding such election, and who have been baptized in the Episcopal church or received therein either by the rite of confirmation or by receiving the holy communion or by purchasing or hiring a pew in said church, or by some joint act of the parties and of the rector, whereby they have attached themselves to the Protestant Episcopal church, and not already incorporated, at any time to meet for the purpose of incorporating themselves under this title, and by a majority of voices to elect two church-wardens and not less than four nor more than eight vestrymen, and to determine on what day of the week called Easter week the said offices of church-wardens and vestrymen shall annually thereafter cease, and their successors in office be chosen; of which first election notice shall be given in the time of morning service on two Sundays previous thereto, by the rector, or if there is none, by any other person belonging to such church or congregation; and that said rector, or if there is none, or he is necessarily absent, then one of the church-wardens or vestrymen, or any other person called to the chair, shall preside at such election, and, together with two other persons, shall make certificate under their hands and seals of the church-wardens and vestrymen so elected, of the day of Easter week so fixed on for the annual election of their successors, and of the name or title by which such church or congregation shall be known in law; which certificate being duly acknowledged, or proved by one or more of the subscribing witnesses before some officer authorized to take acknowledgments of deeds, of the county where such church or place of worship of such congregation is situated, shall be recorded by the clerk of such county in a book to be by him provided for that purpose; and that the church-wardens and vestrymen so elected, and their successors

6

in office, and the rector if any, of themselves shall form a vestry and be the trustees of such church or congregation; and such trustees and their successors shall thereupon, by virtue of this title, be a body corporate by the name and title expressed in such certificate, with all the rights, powers and privileges of other religious corporations constituted according to the provisions of this title; and the persons qualified as aforesaid shall, in every year thereafter, on the day in Easter week so fixed on for that purpose, elect such other church-wardens and vestrymen; and whenever any vacancy happens before the stated annual election, by death or otherwise, the said trustees shall appoint a time for holding an election to supply such vacancy, of which notice shall be given in time of divine service, at least ten days previous thereto; and such election and also the stated annual elections shall be holden immediately after morning service; and at all such elections the rector, or if there is none, or he is absent, one of the church-wardens or vestrymen, shall preside and receive the votes of the electors, and be the returning officer, and shall enter the proceedings in the book of the minutes of the vestry and sign his name thereto, and offer the same to as many electors present as he shall think fit, to be by them also signed and certified; and the church-wardens and vestrymen to be chosen at any of the said elections shall hold their offices until the expiration of the year for which they are chosen and until others are chosen in their stead, and have the power to call and induct a rector to such church or congregation as often as there is a vacancy therein: *Provided, however,* that no meeting or board of such trustees shall be held unless at least three days' notice thereof is given in writing under the hand of the rector or of one of the church-wardens, and that no such board shall be competent to transact any business unless the rector, if there is one, and at least one of the church-wardens and a majority of the vestrymen are present; and such rector, if there is one, and if not, then the church-warden present, or if both the church-wardens are present, then the church-warden who is called to the chair by a majority of voices, shall preside at every such meeting or board and have the casting vote.

CERTIFICATE OF ELECTION AND INCORPORATION.

To all to whom these presents may come: We, whose names are hereunto subscribed, do hereby certify that on the —— day of ——, 18—, the male persons of full age, and who for more than three months last past belonged to (*St. Paul's Church*) of ——, in the State of Minnesota, in communion with the Protestant Episcopal church, having not already been incorporated, met at their church (*or at the residence of H G*) in the —— of ——, in said state, for the purpose of incorporating themselves and electing wardens and vestrymen, in pursuance of notice given by the rector or other person at the time of morning service on two Sundays previous to said meeting, at which meeting Rev. N O, the rector (*or if no rector, S T, warden*), presided, and the undersigned, W X and Y Z, were chosen to act with the said rector or warden in making a certificate of the wardens and vestrymen so elected.

That at said meeting S T and U V were elected wardens, and W X, etc. (*not more than eight*), were elected vestrymen of the said church by a majority of voices. That it was determined by a like vote that their term should cease and their successors in office be annually chosen thereafter on Monday in Easter week; and by a majority vote it was determined by said meeting that the name or title by which such church should be known in law was (*St. Paul's Church*) of ——.

In testimony whereof the said N O, the rector (*or other person who presided*), and W X and Y Z, chosen to make this certificate, have hereunto subscribed our names and affixed our seals this —— day of ——, in the year of our Lord one thousand eight hundred and ——.

N O. [SEAL]
W X. [SEAL]
Y Z. [SEAL]

Signed and sealed in presence of

—— ——
—— ——

NOTE.—For form of acknowledgment see *post*, page 125.

Sec. 24. *Existing societies organized but not incorporated may become incorporated under the provisions of this title.*—Whenever any church or religious society now organized, or which may hereafter be organized, as a church or congregation, but not incorporated in pursuance of law, shall comply with the provisions of this title and thereby become a body corporate, all the estate, real and personal, which has been lawfully conveyed to said church or religious society, or to the trustees or vestry thereof, in trust for the use of such church or society, whether by devise, gift, grant, purchase or otherwise, and not lawfully disposed of, shall thereupon vest in said corporation as fully and amply as if the said church had been legally incorporated from the date of its religious organization: *Provided*, that the name or title publicly assumed or borne by such church or society from the date of its organization as such, and none other, shall be the title by which it shall forever be known in law and as a body politic and corporate.

FORM OF ACKNOWLEDGMENT FOR GENERAL USE.

STATE OF MINNESOTA, }
COUNTY OF ——, } ss.

Be it remembered that on this —— day of ——, 18—, personally came before me A B and C D, to me known to be elders (*deacons, etc., as the case may be*) of —— Church (*or society*), and whose names are subscribed to the foregoing certificate, and then and there acknowledged that they had executed the said certificate freely and voluntarily for the purposes therein expressed and in pursuance of the statute in such case made and provided. —— ——

Justice of the Peace.

CHAPTER XVII.

OHIO STATUTES OF MARRIAGE.

EXPLANATORY.—S. & C., Swan & Crichfield; S. & S., Swan & Saylor; v, volume, as 73 v, 224 p.

Section 1. Male persons of the age of eighteen years, and female persons of the age of sixteen years, not nearer of kin than second cousins, and not having
67 v, 6] a husband or wife living, may be joined in marriage: *Provided always*, that male persons under the age of twenty-one years, and female persons under the age of eighteen years, shall first obtain the consent of their fathers respectively, or in case of the death or incapacity of their fathers, then of their mothers or guardians.

Sec. 2. Any ordained minister of any religious society or congregation within this state, who has or may hereafter obtain a license for that purpose, as here-
S. & C. 855] inafter provided, or any justice of the peace in his county, or the several religious societies, may, agreeably to the rules and regulations of their respective churches, join together as husband and wife all persons not prohibited by this act.

Sec. 3. Any minister of the gospel, upon producing

to the probate judge of any county within this state in which he officiates, credentials of his being a regular ordained minister of any religious society or congregation, shall be entitled to receive from said judge a license authorizing him to solemnize marriages within this state so long as he shall continue a regular minister in such society or congregation.

Sec. 4. It shall be the duty of every minister who is now or hereafter shall be licensed to solemnize marriages as aforesaid, to produce to the probate judge in every county in which he shall solemnize any marriage his license so obtained, and the said judge shall thereupon enter the name of such minister upon record as a minister of the gospel duly authorized to solemnize marriages within this state, and shall note the county from which such license issued, for which service no charge shall be [made] by such judge.

Sec. 5. When the name of any such minister is so entered upon the record by the judge aforesaid, such record, or the certificate thereof by the said judge under the seal of his office, shall be good evidence that the said minister was duly authorized to solemnize marriages.

Sec. 6. Previous to persons being joined in marriage notice thereof shall be published (in the presence of the congregation) on two different days of public worship; the first publication to be at least ten days previous to such marriage, within the county where the female resides, or a license shall be obtained for that purpose from the probate judge in the county where such female may reside.

Sec. 7. The probate judge, as aforesaid, may inquire of the party applying for marriage license, as aforesaid, upon oath or affirmation, relative to the legality of such contemplated marriage, and if the judge shall be satisfied there is no legal impediment thereto, then he shall grant such marriage license; and if any of the persons intending to marry shall be under age, and shall not have had a former wife or husband, the consent of the parent or guardian shall be personally given before the judge, or certified under the hand of such parent or guardian, attested by two witnesses, one of which shall appear before said judge and make oath or affirmation that he saw the parent or guardian whose name is annexed to such certificate subscribe, or heard him or her acknowledge the same; and the judge is hereby authorized to administer such oath or affirmation, and thereupon issue and sign such license and affix thereto the seal of the court.

Sec. 8. A certificate of every marriage hereafter solemnized, signed by the justice or minister solemniz-
S. & S. 447] ing the same, where the marriage license was issued, shall be transmitted to the probate judge of the county where the marriage license was issued within three months thereafter, and recorded by such probate judge. Every justice or minister (as the case may be) failing to transmit such certificate to the probate judge in due time shall forfeit and pay fifty dollars; and if the probate judge shall neglect to make such record he shall forfeit and pay fifty dollars to and for the use of the county.

NOTE.—*Such certificate may be as follows:*

COUNTY OF ——,
CITY (*or Town*) OF ——, } SS.

I hereby certify that on the —— day of ——, 18—, at the dwelling house of T D (*or at the* —— *Church*), in the town (*or city*) of ——, in the State of Ohio, I joined in the bonds of holy matrimony Mr. C D, of ——, county of ——, in said state, and Miss E F, of (*etc.*), they having produced to me a license issued by the probate judge of the county of ——, being the county in which such female resided (*or being satisfied that notice of such intended marriage had been published according to law; and if either the man is under the age of twenty-one years, or the woman under the age of eighteen years, and shall not have had a former wife or husband, and no license is produced, then say*) that the consent of the father (*or mother, or guardian, as the case may be*) of Mr. C D (*or Miss E F*) was given in my presence (*or was obtained in writing*), as appears by a certificate under the hand of L M, the father (*or guardian*) of said C D (*or E F*), attested by L D, who was present for that purpose.

Dated at —— this —— day of ——, 18—.

S F,
Rector (*or Pastor*).

Sec. 9. If any justice or minister by this act authorized to join persons in marriage, shall solemnize the S. & C. 855] same contrary to the true intent and meaning of this act, the person so offending shall upon conviction thereof forfeit and pay any sum not exceeding one thousand dollars, to and for the use of the county wherein such offense was committed. And if any person not legally authorized shall attempt to solemnize the marriage contract such person shall upon conviction thereof forfeit and pay five hundred dollars to and for the use of the county wherein such offense was committed.

NOTE.—Under this provision of the statute a minister or justice solemnizing a marriage of persons not having a license or not having bans properly published, and not having had a former husband or wife, the man being under twenty-one years of age, or the woman under eighteen, and shall not procure the consent of parents or guardians; or if a minister who has not filed his credentials of ordination with the probate judge, and not having received a license, would incur this penalty. But when a license is produced from the probate judge in proper form, this is all that the minister need look to, the question of bans or of the age of the parties cannot be inquired into, the responsibility is then with the probate judge.

Sec. 10. Every minister or justice of the peace, before he shall solemnize any marriage between the parties, either of whom is required by the first section of this act to obtain the consent of his or her parent or guardian (except in cases where license shall have been obtained from the probate judge), must be satisfied that the intention of marriage between such parties has been duly published, and also that the consent of such parent or guardian has been obtained, either by acknowledgment in presence of such minister or justice of the peace, or by a certificate under the signature of such parent or guardian and attested by one or more credible witnesses who shall be present for the purpose of satisfying such minister or justice of the peace that such certificate was actually signed by the parent or guardian for the purpose aforesaid.

NOTE.—The consent, if in writing, may be in the following form:

I, J S, of (*Cleveland*), in the State of Ohio, the father (*or mother*) of G S, who is under the age of twenty-one years (*or C D, who is under the age of eighteen years*), do hereby consent that the said G S may be joined in marriage with Miss C D (*or that the said C D, who is under the age of eighteen years, may be joined in marriage with Mr. G S, according to the facts*).

Dated at ——, etc. J S.

Attest: L M, H G, } Witnesses present.

Sec. 11. Any fine or forfeiture arising to the county in consequence of the breach of this act shall be recovered by an action of debt, with costs of suit, in any court of such county having cognizance of the same.

NOTE.—The marriage ceremony may be regarded either as a civil ceremony or as a religious sacrament. The law prescribes no particular form of marriage ceremony. (For form see *ante*, pages 26 and 27.)

Sec. 12. It shall be unlawful for any person of pure white blood to intermarry with or have illicit carnal
S. & S. 267] intercourse with any negro, or person having a distinct and visible admixture of African blood, or for any negro or person having a distinct and visible admixture of African blood to intermarry with or have illicit carnal intercourse with any person of pure white blood; and any person offending against either of the provisions of this section shall be deemed guilty of a misdemeanor, and on conviction thereof shall be fined in any sum not exceeding one hundred dollars, or be imprisoned in the jail of the county for any period not exceeding three months, or both, at the discretion of the court.

Sec. 13. Any person who shall knowingly solemnize a marriage forbidden by previous sections of this act, or any probate judge who shall knowingly issue a license for the solemnization of any marriage forbidden by this act, shall be deemed guilty of a misdemeanor, and on conviction thereof shall be fined in any sum not exceeding one hundred dollars, or imprisonment in the county jail for a period not exceeding three months, or both, at the discretion of the court.

NOTE.—See note, page 76, *ante*.

CHAPTER XVIII.

OHIO STATUTES OF RELIGIOUS ASSEMBLIES.

Section 1. If any person or persons shall at any time interrupt or molest any religious society, or per-
73 v, 224] sons when meeting or met together for the purpose of worship, or performing any duties enjoined on or appertaining to them as members of such society, or shall so interrupt or molest any such society, member or person at any time during the period that he, she or they may remain at or about the place where such meeting is to be, is or has been held, the person or persons so offending shall be deemed guilty of a misdemeanor, and upon conviction thereof shall be fined in any sum not exceeding fifty dollars, or imprisoned in the proper county jail for any period not exceeding ten days, or both, at the discretion of the court: *Provided*, that this section shall not be so construed as to deprive any religious society of the right of laying hands upon the person or persons who may be disturbing the congregation, and turning him, her or them out of the church or place of worship.

Sec. 2. No person shall sell or expose for sale, give, barter or otherwise dispose of, in any way, or at any
S. & S. 288] place, any spirituous or other liquors, or any articles of traffic whatsoever, at or within the distance

of four miles from the place where any religious society or assemblage of people are collected or collecting together for religious worship in any field or woodland: *Provided*, that nothing in this act shall affect tavern keepers exercising their calling; nor distillers, manufacturers or others in prosecuting their regular trades at their places of business, or any person disposing of any ordinary articles of provisions, excepting spirituous liquors, at their residences; nor any person having a written permit from the trustees or managers of any such religious society or assemblage to sell provisions for the supply of persons attending such religious worship, their horses or cattle, such persons acting in conformity to the regulations of said religious assembly and to the laws of the state.

Sec. 3. Any person found guilty of committing a breach of the provisions of this act shall forfeit and
S. & C. 453] pay for every such offense a fine of not less than ten nor more than one hundred dollars into the township treasury for the use of the common schools in said township where said offense was committed; and any judge of the common pleas, sheriff, coroner or justice of the peace of the county, or any constable thereof, shall, upon view or information, and with or without warrant, apprehend any person so offending, and seize all such liquors or other articles of traffic, and the utensils or furniture containing them, and convey them before a justice of the peace; and the said justice, upon the complaint under oath or affirmation of said officer apprehending such offender, or any person giving information, shall issue his warrant of arrest,

which shall be formally served by the proper officer, and proceed to inquire into the truth of said accusation, and, if found true, shall proceed to bind said offender in such amount not exceeding five hundred dollars as he shall deem proper to answer at the next regular term of the common pleas in said county, to be proceeded with by indictment, the fine and costs to be collected as in other criminal cases: *Provided*, that if such defendant or defendants shall plead guilty, said justice shall affix the penalty and proceed to judgment; and in such case he shall immediately issue an execution against the property and body of the defendant or defendants for the fine and costs unless paid or secured; and said defendant or defendants shall not be discharged until said judgment and costs shall be fully paid or secured to be paid.

Sec. 4. If any person of the age of fourteen years or upward shall be found on the first day of the week, **S. & S. 289**] commonly called Sunday, sporting, rioting, quarreling, hunting, fishing or shooting, he or she shall be fined in a sum not exceeding twenty dollars, or be confined in the county jail for a term not exceeding twenty days, or both, at the discretion of the court. And if any person of the age of fourteen years or upward shall be found on the first day of the week, commonly called Sunday, at common labor (works of necessity and charity only excepted), he or she shall be fined in a sum not exceeding five dollars nor less than one dollar: *Provided*, nothing herein contained in relation to common labor on said first day of the week, commonly called Sunday, shall be construed to extend to those who conscientiously do observe the seventh day of the week as the Sabbath, nor to prevent families emigrating from traveling, watermen from landing their passengers, superintendents or keepers of toll bridges or toll gates from attending and superintending the same, or ferrymen from conveying travelers over the water, or persons moving their families on such days.

EXTRACT FROM CONSTITUTION OF OHIO.

Sec. 5. All men have a natural and indefeasible right to worship Almighty God according to the dictates of their own conscience. No person shall be compelled to attend, erect or support any place of worship or maintain any form of worship against his consent, and no preference shall be given by law to any religious society, nor shall any interference with the rights of conscience be permitted. No religious test shall be required as a qualification for office, nor shall any person be incompetent to be a witness on account of his religious belief; but nothing herein shall be construed to dispense with oaths and affirmations. Religion, morality and knowledge, however, being essential to good government, it shall be the duty of the general assembly to pass suitable laws to protect every religious denomination in the peaceable enjoyment of its own mode of public worship, and to encourage schools and the means of instruction.

DUTIES OF CLERGYMEN.

Sec. 6. It shall be the duty of clergymen who have officiated at the funeral and who have buried deceased
68 v, 49] persons to keep a registry of the name, age

and residence of such deceased persons, at the time of their death, and to report fully the deaths registered by them as required by this act to the judge of the probate court of the county every three months as above designated; and any person who shall neglect or refuse to comply with or [shall] violate the provisions of this act, shall forfeit and pay for each offense the sum of ten dollars, to be sued for and recovered in the name of the State of Ohio, and the penalty when recovered shall be paid over, one half to the school fund and one half to the party making complaint thereof.

Sec. 7. All clergymen within any municipal corporation, and all other persons authorized to solemnize
71 v, 159] marriages, shall keep a registry of all marriages solemnized by them, and shall report to the board of health all such marriages occurring within the limits of such city as registered by them, and such report shall be made as often as the board of health may require; and any person or persons who shall neglect or refuse to comply with or shall violate any of the foregoing provisions shall forfeit and pay for each offense in any sum not exceeding fifty dollars, to be sued for and recovered in the police court of such city in the name of the State of Ohio, and said court is hereby vested with jurisdiction in such cases.

Sec. 8. All clergymen and priests shall be incompetent to testify concerning any confession made to
67 v, 113] them in their professional character in the course of discipline enjoined by the church to which they belong, without the consent of the person making the confession. And all clergymen and priests shall be exempt from serving on juries.

CHAPTER XIX.

OHIO STATUTES OF RELIGIOUS SOCIETIES.

Section 1. It shall be lawful for any religious sect, denomination or association, fire company, or any liter-
S. & S. 239] ary, scientific or benevolent association, other than colleges, universities, academies or seminaries within this state, or having a central or principal place of meeting or business therein, to elect at a meeting of a majority of any organized synod, presbytery, conference, convention, church, parish, or other religious or ministerial association, fire company, literary, scientific or benevolent association, as aforesaid, any number of their members, not less than three, to serve as trustees or directors, who shall hold their office during the pleasure of the society or association: *Provided*, that when any such synod, presbytery, conference, convention, church, parish or other religious association aforesaid has heretofore elected any number of persons, not less than three, to serve as directors or trustees, holding their office during the pleasure of such society or association, such persons shall be invested with the powers, privileges and immunities granted by the provisions of this act, upon there being recorded by the recorder of the proper county a proper cetificate of the

election of such persons, and the corporate name given to the same by such synod, presbytery, conference, church, parish or other religious association, to be made by its clerk, secretary, or other like officer, together with a certificate of the said directors or trustees, or a majority of them, of their acceptance of the provisions of this act; *or provided*, that where by the laws or regulations of any such synod, presbytery, conference, convention, church, parish or other association aforesaid, now or hereafter organized, any members thereof, less than three, have charge of the property or concerns thereof, such less number of members and their successors shall be invested with the powers, privileges and immunities granted to three trustees or directors by the provisions of this act, upon there being recorded by the recorder of the proper county a proper certificate of the election of such members, and the corporate name adopted by such synod, presbytery, conference, convention, church, parish or other association, to be made by their clerk, secretary or other like officer.

FORM OF CERTIFICATE.

STATE OF OHIO, }
COUNTY OF ——. } SS.

I hereby certify that at a meeting of a majority of the members of the synod (*presbytery, conference, etc., as the case may be*), held at their house of worship (*or at the dwelling house of* —— ——), in the town of ——, county of ——, and State of Ohio, on the —— day of ——, 18—, pursuant to notice, for the election of trustees (*or directors*), Messrs. T D, L E and O P (*not less than three*) were duly elected such trustees (*or directors*), and it was determined at such meeting, by a majority vote, that the corporate name by which said church (*or society*) should thereafter be known and called be (*here give the name*) Church (*or Society*), of ——.

Given under my hand at ——, this —— day of ——, 18—.

—— ——,
Clerk (*or Secretary*).

ACCEPTANCE.

We, and each of us, whose names are hereunder written, do accept of the office of trustees (*or directors*) to which we have been elected, as appears by the above certificate, and take upon ourselves the responsibilities of the same.

Dated ——, 18—.

T D,
L E,
O P.

Sec. 2. The clerk, secretary, or like officer, shall make a true record of the proceedings of the meeting provided for by the preceding section of this act, certify and deliver the same to the recorder of the county in which such meeting shall be held, or in which the principal property of such church, fire company, synod, presbytery, conference, convention, parish or other religious or benevolent association shall be situated, or in which their principal enterprise or business is carried on, together with the name by which such church, fire company, synod, presbytery, conference, convention, parish or other religious or benevolent association shall thereafter desire to be known; and it shall be the duty of such county recorder, immediately upon the receipt of such certified statement, to record the same in a book of record to be kept by him, provided for that purpose at the expense of his county, for which service he may demand and receive the sum of ten cents per hundred words; and from and after making such record by the county recorder, the said trustees or directors and their associated members and successors shall be invested with the power, privileges and immunities incident to aggregate corporations; and a certified transcript of the record herein authorized to be made by the county recorder shall be deemed and taken in all courts and places whatsoever in this state as evidence of the existence of such association and corporation.

Sec. 3. If said board of trustees or directors, as provided for by the first section of this act, shall be vacated, either in whole or in part, by death, resignation or otherwise, such board of trustees or directors may be revived, or such vacancy or vacancies filled in the manner pointed out in the first section of this act for the original organization of said board, or in the manner pointed out by the laws and regulations of such religious or benevolent associations, and a majority of said trustees or directors shall be a quorum for the transaction of business.

Sec. 4. The trustees or directors who may be appointed under the provisions of this act, and their successors in office, shall have perpetual succession by S. & C. 308] such name as may be designated, and by such name shall be legally capable of contracting and of prosecuting and defending suits, and shall have capacity to acquire, hold, enjoy, dispose of and convey all property, real or personal, which they may acquire by purchase, donation or otherwise for the purpose of carrying out the intentions of such society or association, but they shall not acquire or hold property for any other purpose.

Sec. 5. Such society or association when incorporated may elect such officers, and make such rules and regulations as may be necessary and expedient for its own government and the management of its fiscal and other affairs to affect their respective objects.

Sec. 6. When any real estate shall have or may hereafter be bequeathed, purchased, donated or other-
S. & C. 371] wise intrusted to any religious society in this state, or to any of the trustees or officers of any such society, for the use and benefit of any such society, or for any other purpose, and such society shall be desirous to sell, exchange or incumber by mortgage or otherwise any such real estate, it shall be lawful for the court of common pleas of the proper county, upon good cause shown upon petition of any such society, or some person authorized by them, to make an order authorizing the sale or incumbrance of any such real estate, and said court may include in such order directions how the proceeds of such sale or incumbrance shall be appropriated or invested: *Provided*, such order shall in no case be inconsistent with the original terms upon which such real estate became invested in or intrusted to such religious society.

Sec. 7. Where any religious society shall petition

as is provided for in the preceding section, all persons who may have a vested contingent or a reversionary interest in the real estate sought to be sold or incumbered shall be made parties to said petition, and such parties shall be notified of such petition in the same manner as is or may be provided for in cases of petition for partition of real estate: *Provided*, that the provisions of this act shall not extend to any grounds used or occupied as burial-places for the dead.

Sec. 8. Whenever any religious society shall desire to sell any real estate that may have been conveyed to
S. & S. 163] such society and is held in trust for a specified religious purpose, it shall be lawful for the trustees, wardens and vestry, or other officers intrusted with the management of the affairs of such society, to file in the court of common pleas of the county where such real estate may be situated a petition stating that such society desires to make such sale, setting forth the object of such sale; and if upon the hearing of such case it shall appear that such sale is desired by the members of such society, and that there is a necessity for the same, the court may authorize the trustees or other officers holding the title in trust to sell said real estate in such manner and upon such terms as the court shall deem reasonable.

Sec. 9. The trustees or other officers authorized to make such sale shall make return thereof to the court ordering the same at such time as the court shall order; and thereupon, if the court shall be satisfied that the same has been made in all respects according to its order, and that the proceeds have been invested in other real estate for the use of such society, or otherwise invested or disposed of according to the wish of such society, the said sale shall be confirmed and a deed authorized to be made to the purchaser: *Provided*, that the provisions of this act shall not extend to any grounds used or occupied as burial-places for the dead.

Sec. 10. The petitioners shall cause notice of the pendency and prayer of the petition to be published S. & C. 372] for four consecutive weeks in some newspaper of general circulation in the county where the real estate proposed to be sold is situate before the term of the court at which the order of sale will be asked.

Sec. 11. It shall be lawful for any religious society incorporated under any of the general laws or any S. & S. 162] special law of this state, and which act of incorporation prescribes that the public religious services of such society shall be conducted in any other than the English language, at any time by a vote of the majority of the adult members in good and regular standing of such society, who speak such prescribed language, to decide whether the public religious services of said society may at any time be conducted in any other than the prescribed language.

UNION OF TWO OR MORE RELIGIOUS SOCIETIES.

Sec. 12. Whenever two or more religious societies, churches or associations, recognizing the same eccle-67 v, 30] siastical jurisdiction, form of faith, government, order and discipline, and incorporated by or under any law of the state, shall desire to become consolidated or united as a single corporation, it shall be lawful for the elders, trustees, deacons, directors, or other known and legal representatives of such two or more societies, churches or associations, to enter into an agreement for such union or consolidation, to prescribe the terms and conditions thereof, the corporate name of such united society, church or association, the time and place for the first meeting of the new corporation, the number of each separate branch or organization who shall be chosen as directors, trustees, elders or other officers for the new corporation, to succeed to the rights, trusts, duties and obligations of those officers who in the separate organizations held in trust the estate, real and personal, of such separate churches, societies or associations, with such other estates as they shall deem necessary to complete such new corporation: *Provided*, that all agreements so made as aforesaid shall not be conclusive and valid until said agreement, with its terms, shall have been submitted to a meeting, of which due and full notice shall be given according to the form and usage for calling church, congregation or society meetings of the members of each separate organization, and shall have been ratified by a two-thirds vote of all present at said meeting, in person or by proxy, and entitled to vote according to the laws, regulations or usages of such church, society or corporation.

Sec. 13. That whenever said agreement shall have been ratified as aforesaid by each church, society or association, a party to said proposed united organization, the clerk or secretary of said several and respective meetings shall certify the record of the proceedings of said meeting, and deliver the same to the clerk or secretary of the first meeting of the united churches, societies or organizations, as hereinbefore provided and as specified in said terms of agreement.

Sec. 14. At the aforesaid first meeting, as provided for in the terms of agreement, the proceedings and acts of the several churches, societies, and parties thereto, shall have been submitted and approved by said meeting, and a board of trustees, directors or other officers shall have been chosen in accordance with the aforesaid terms of agreement. The clerk or secretary of said meeting shall certify such approved agreement or terms of union to the recorder of the county in which such united church shall be situated, which shall be recorded as provided for by law; and upon the filing of said certificate the several church societies or associations, parties thereto, shall be deemed and taken to be one corporation, possessing within this state all the rights, privileges and franchises, and subject to all the restrictions, disabilities and duties of such new corporation of the state so united.

Sec. 15. Such new corporation constituted as aforesaid, with its officers and chosen representatives, shall succeed to and shall be invested with all and singular the right, title and interest in and to every species of property, real, personal or mixed, and all and singular the rights, privileges and franchises of each of said churches, societies or associations, parties to the same, without any other act, conveyance or transfer whatsoever; and such new corporation shall hold and enjoy the same with all the rights pertaining to such property, franchises and trusts; and such new corporation shall be subject to all the debts, liabilities and obligations in the same manner and to the same extent as any or either of said churches or societies, parties to the new corporation.

TO CONVEY REAL ESTATE.

Sec. 16. Whenever any two or more religious societies, denominations or ecclesiastical corporations in
73 v, 225] this state shall hereafter unanimously form, or have heretofore unanimously formed, a union, and become united or consolidated under and by virtue of any rules and regulations of any such societies, denominations or corporations, or laws of this state, then it shall be lawful for the trustees, deacons, directors or other proper officers of such new society, denomination or corporation formed as aforesaid, to petition the court of common pleas of the proper county, at the request of a majority of the members of any such society, denomination or corporation, setting forth the fact of such union as aforesaid; and said court may in its discretion make an order requiring said trustees, deacons, directors or such other proper officers, at the time of such union of any such societies, denominations or ecclesiastical corporations forming the same, to convey the real estate owned and held by such religious society, denomination or corporation forming such union, to such new organization as the court may direct; and in case any of such trustees, deacons, directors or other officers as aforesaid shall refuse or neglect to obey such order,

then, in that case, the decree of such court shall act as such conveyancer: *Provided*, such order shall in no case be inconsistent with the original terms upon which such real estate became invested in or intrusted to such societies, denominations or corporations; and in all cases the grantors of such real estate to such societies, denominations or corporations, or their heirs, shall be made parties to the petition; *and provided further*, that such grantors or their heirs who make no defense shall not be subject to costs.

Sec. 17. Notice of the pendency of such petition shall be by publication in a newspaper printed and published in the county where such petition is filed for four consecutive weeks, setting forth the object and prayer of said petition, and in the event no newspaper is printed in the county where such petition is filed, then such publication shall be made in the newspaper published nearest to said county.

Sec. 18. When any real estate shall have been or may hereafter be donated or bequeathed to or purchased by, or otherwise intrusted to any person or
66 v, 126] persons, trustee or trustees, for any public religious use, but not to or for the use of any specific or particular religious society or denomination, or when the same has been or may be to a particular religious society or denomination, and shall have been abandoned for such use, it shall be lawful for the court of common pleas of the county in which the same is located, upon good cause shown, upon the petition of any citizen or citizens of the vicinity, to make an order for the sale of such property, whether the same shall

have been built upon or otherwise improved or not, and may order such disposition of the proceeds of such sale to such religious or other public use as shall be just, proper and equitable; and the purchaser or purchasers thereof shall be invested with as full and complete title to said property as the character of the original grant for such religious use will allow.

Sec. 19. When any petition shall be filed as provided for in the preceding section, all persons who may have a vested contingent or reversionary interest in such real estate, and the trustees or other temporal officers of any religious society then using said real estate, shall be made parties to said petition, and be notified of the filing and pendency thereof in the same manner as is or may be provided in case of partition of real estate: *Provided*, that the provisions of this act shall not authorize the sale or transfer of burial-grounds or cemetery; *and provided also*, that said court shall have power to make such order as to costs as shall be deemed just and proper.

NOTE.—The following laws relating to religious societies, etc., passed prior to the adoption of the constitution of 1851, and prior to the foregoing enactments, are found in the statute of Swan and Crichfield, pages 305 to 308.

ACT OF MARCH 5, 1836.

Sec. 20. Any religious society hereafter incorporated by an act of the legislature shall have perpetual succession by such name as may be designated, and by such name shall be legally capable of contracting and of prosecuting and defending suits, and shall have capacity to acquire, hold, enjoy and dispose of a house for public worship with the land necessary therefor, not exceeding in quantity one acre, a burying-ground for such society, a parsonage not exceeding in value the sum of five thousand dollars, and any other property not exceeding in value the sum of five thousand dollars, and any other property not exceeding the annual value of one thousand dollars, which shall be applied to the support of public worship and such institutions of learning and charity as may be connected with such society, and to no other purpose.

Sec. 21. Such society when incorporated may elect such officers and make such rules as may be necessary and expedient for its own government and the management of its affairs.

Sec. 22. Mesne process shall be served on the corporation by leaving an attested copy thereof with any one of its officers at least ten days before the return day thereof.

Sec. 23. The legislature may at any time repeal or alter an act incorporating any religious society, but no rights granted or acquired by proceedings under the said acts shall be affected by the repeal, nor shall associations constituted and organized under such acts be dissolved or in any way affected by such repeal.

ACT OF JANUARY 3, 1825.

Sec. 24. All lands and tenements not exceeding twenty acres, that have been or hereafter may be conveyed by devise, purchase or otherwise to any person or persons as trustee or trustees, in trust for the use of any religious society within this state, either for a meeting-house, burying-ground or residence for their preacher, shall descend, with the improvements and appurtenances, in perpetual succession, in trust to such trustee or trustees as shall from time to time be elected or appointed by any such religious society according to the rules and regulations of such society respectively.

Sec. 25. The trustee or trustees for the time being of any religious society aforesaid shall have the same power to defend and prosecute suits at law or in equity, and do all other acts for the protection, improvement and preservation of said property, as individuals may do in relation to their individual property.

ACT OF MARCH 12, 1844.

Sec. 26. From and after the passage of this act it shall be lawful for any religious society within this state (at a meeting of a majority of the members of any organized society thereof, called for that purpose, of which meeting notice shall have been first given by posting up written or printed advertisements in three of the most public places in the township in which said society may be) to elect any number of their members, not less than three, to serve as trustees, and one member to serve as clerk, who shall hold their offices during the pleasure of said society.

Sec. 27. The clerk hereinbefore authorized to be appointed shall forthwith make out a true record of the proceedings of the meeting provided for by the previous section of this act, certify and deliver the same to the recorder of the county in which such meeting shall be held, together with the name by which such church shall thereafter desire to be known; and it shall be the duty of each county recorder in this state, immediately upon the receipt of such certified statement, to record the same in a book of record, to be by him provided for that purpose at the expense of his county, for which service he may demand and receive from the person presenting the same a compensation at the rate of six cents for each hundred words; and from and after making such record by the county recorder the said trustees and their associated members and successors shall be invested with the powers, privileges and immunities incident to aggregate corporations; and a certified transcript of the record herein authorized to be made by the county recorder shall be deemed and taken in all courts and places whatsoever within this state as conclusive evidence of the existence of such associated religious society.

Sec. 28. The trustees who may be appointed under the provisions of this act shall have perpetual succession, and shall possess all and singular the powers and privileges granted to, and shall be subject to all the restrictions imposed upon the corporators of religious societies by an act entitled "An act in relation to incorporated religious societies," passed March fifth, one thousand eight hundred and thirty-six; and also the act entitled "An act securing to religious societies a perpetuity of title to lands and tenements conveyed in trust for meeting-houses, burying-grounds or residences of preachers," passed January third, one thousand eight hundred and twenty-five, so far as such acts are not inconsistent with the provisions of this act.

Sec. 29. If said board of trustees, as provided for

by this act, shall be vacated either in whole or in part, by death, refusal to serve, or otherwise, such board of trustees may be revived, or such vacancy or vacancies filled in the same manner as is pointed out in this act for the original creation or organization of said board, and a majority of said board of trustees shall be a quorum for the transaction of business.

Sec. 30. So much of the act entitled "An act in relation to incorporated religious societies," passed March fifth, one thousand eight hundred and thirty-six, as is inconsistent with this act be and the same is hereby repealed.

ACT OF FEBRUARY 28, 1846.

Sec. 31. Where any religious, literary or other society has been or may be incorporated by any act of the general assembly, and a certain day appointed by such act for the annual election of the officers of such society, and any such society have neglected, or shall neglect, to elect their proper officers on such day, such neglect shall not work any dissolution of such incorporations; but the officers of such society last elected shall exercise the duties of their respective offices until their successors are elected and qualified.

Sec. 32. Whenever any such society shall neglect to elect their officers on the day appointed for their annual election by their act of incorporation, or shall neglect to organize on the day fixed by said act, it shall be lawful for any three members of such society to call a meeting by a written notice put up at three of the most public places in the vicinity of the place where such society usually hold their meetings, at least ten days before the time for the meeting thereby called, stating the object of such meeting, at which time and place it shall be lawful for such society to elect officers in the same manner as they should have done at their last annual election, or to organize in the manner pointed out in the charter, as if there had been no failure to elect on the day specified in the charter; and such officers thus elected shall hold their offices until the next annual election and until their successors are elected and qualified.

Sec. 33. It shall be lawful for any religious, literary or other societies, incorporated by any special act of the general assembly, who have organized under the same and acquired any property, whenever such society choose to do so, to organize under any general law of this state for the purpose of incorporating such societies without any special act of incorporation, and upon such organization such society shall have, hold and enjoy all property which they acquired and held under their former act of incorporation.

ACT OF MARCH 23, 1850.

Sec. 34. Whenever any property has been or may be conveyed in trust for the use of any religious society, church or association, whether incorporated or not, the property so conveyed shall be held by the trustee or trustees so appointed, and their successors, appointed as provided in the instrument creating such trust, or in case no provision is made in such instrument, then by such successor or successors as may be appointed by any competent court; but no person shall be elected or appointed by such society, church or association to act as trustees to the exclusion of any trustee or trustees appointed as aforesaid.

NOTE.—The following acts relate to religious societies, but are not printed here in full as they seem to apply to special cases:

An act to authorize Presbyterian churches or societies which have been incorporated, to elect deacons to serve as trustees. (S. & C. 307.)

An act to provide for the incorporation of printing and publishing houses by religious denominations. (68 v, 43.)

An act to regulate the sale of certain real estate held in trust for a specified religious purpose (S. & S. 163), also property unappropriated (S. & S. 164 and 165).

An act to provide for the sale of lands within any incorporated city or village which have been used for cemetery purposes. (S. & S. 164.)

An act relating to the partition of real estate held in common by two or more religious societies. (S. & C. 371.)

CHAPTER XX.

WISCONSIN STATUTES OF MARRIAGE.

Section 1. Marriage, so far as its validity in law is concerned, is a civil contract, to which the consent of the parties capable in law of contracting is essential.

Sec. 2. Every male person who shall have attained the full age of eighteen years, and every female who shall have attained the full age of fifteen years, shall be capable in law of contracting marriage if otherwise competent.

Sec. 3. No marriage shall be contracted whilst either of the parties has a husband or wife living, nor between parties who are nearer of kin than first cousins, computing by the rules of civil law, whether of the half or of the whole blood, and no insane person or idiot shall be capable of contracting marriage.

Sec. 4. Marriages may be solemnized by any justice of the peace in the county in which he is elected, and they may be solemnized throughout the state by any judge of a court of record, and by any ordained minister of the gospel in regular communion with any religious society, and who continues to be a preacher of the gospel, and by court commissioners.

Sec. 5. Ministers of the gospel, before they shall be authorized to perform the marriage rite, shall file a copy of their credentials of ordination with the clerk of the circuit court of some county in this state, who shall record the same and give a certificate thereof; and the place where such credentials are recorded shall be indorsed upon each certificate of marriage granted by any minister, and recorded with the same.

Sec. 6. All judges, justices of the peace and ministers of the gospel shall, before solemnizing any marriage, examine at least one of the parties on oath, which oath they are hereby authorized to administer, as to the legality of such intended marriage; and in no case shall such judge, justice or minister solemnize a marriage unless he is satisfied from such examination that there is no legal impediment thereto.

NOTE.—A neglect to examine one of the parties on oath, according to this section, might subject the officiating minister to the penalty provided in sections ten and eleven; and simply swearing one of the parties, and asking him or her whether they know of any legal impediment to the marriage is not enough. The statute requires that "he shall examine at least one of the parties" on oath. When that is done, if the party makes a false statement, the officiating minister is not responsible, provided he has reason to believe such statement to be true and is satisfied that it is true; but if it plainly appears that there is a legal impediment to such marriage, and he performs the ceremony, he acts willfully, and would be liable to the penalty.

No magistrate or minister is obliged to perform the marriage ceremony in any given case; he can decline if he chooses.

The following is a proper form of oath to be administered to the party holding up the right hand, or by any other form to him most binding that he may choose.

You do solemnly swear (*or affirm, if the party prefer it*) that you will true answers make to such questions as shall be put to you touching the legality of your intended marriage with Miss E R: So help you God.

Of course any questions may be put after this oath has been administered that may be pertinent or proper, but the following are suggested in order to bring out the facts necessary to enable the officiating minister to make the certificate required of him by section two of chapter one hundred and ten of the Revised Statutes (Sec. 14, *post*); and it is recommended that blanks be provided with the interrogatories printed, so that the answers may be written opposite as they are given, viz.:

What is your full name?
What is the full name of your father?
What is the full name of your mother?
What is your occupation?
What is the name of your place of residence?
What is the name of your birthplace?
What is the full name of this woman?
What is the full name of her father?
What is the full name of her mother?
What is your age?
What is the age of this woman?
Have either of you ever been married?
If so, have either of you a husband or wife living?
Are you related to each other either by consanguinity or affinity?
If so, what is the relation?
Do you know of any legal impediment to your being joined in marriage with this woman?
If the man is under twenty-one or the woman under the age of eighteen years, the following:
Have you or either of you parents living in this state, or have either of you a guardian in this state?
And if so, have you or either of you the written consent of such parents or guardian?

Sec. 7. If any person intending to marry shall be under the age of twenty-one years, if a male, or under the age of eighteen years, if a female, and shall not have had a former wife or husband, the consent in person or in writing of the parent or guardian having the custody of such minor, if he or she have either a parent or guardian living in this state, shall first be given to the person solemnizing the marriage, before such marriage shall take place; and if such consent is in writing it shall be signed by the parent or guardian, and attested by two witnesses, one of whom shall appear and make oath before the person who shall solemnize the marriage that he saw such parent or guardian execute the same.

NOTE.—The consent, if in writing, may be in the following form:

I, J S, the parent (*or guardian*) of G S, who is under the age of twenty-one years, do hereby consent that the said G S may be joined in matrimony with C D. J S.

In presence of
L M,
H G.

AFFIDAVIT OF ONE OF THE WITNESSES.

——— COUNTY, SS.

L M, being duly sworn, says that he saw J S, the parent (*or guardian*) of G S, execute the above or annexed certificate of consent that G S might be joined in the bonds of matrimony with Miss C D, and that he signed said certificate as a subscribing witness thereto. L M.

Subscribed and sworn to before me this —— day of ——, 18—.

R S,
Justice of the Peace.

Sec. 8. In the solemnization of marriage no particular form shall be required, except that the parties shall solemnly declare in the presence of the judge, minister or magistrate, and the attending witnesses, that they take each other as husband and wife; and in every case there shall be at least two witnesses present besides the person performing the ceremony.

NOTE.—For appropriate marriage ceremony see *ante*, pages 26 and 27.

Sec. 9. Whenever a marriage shall have been solemnized, the person solemnizing the same shall give to each of the parties, if requested, a certificate thereof, specifying therein the names and residence of the parties, and of at least two of the witnesses present, and the time and place of such marriage, and also stating therein that he had examined on oath one or both of the parties and found no legal impediment to their marriage, and, where the consent of the parent or guardian is necessary, stating that the same was duly given.

MARRIAGE CERTIFICATE.

This is to certify that Mr. G S, of the (*city of Madison*), in the county of (*Dane*) and State of Wisconsin, and Miss C D, of the same place (*or of Watertown*), in said State, were on the —— day of ——, 18—, joined in holy matrimony by me at the residence of —— ——, (*or at* —— *Church*), in the city of (*Milwaukee*) in said State, in the presence of L M, of (*Milwaukee*), and H G, of (*Madison*) aforesaid, among others as attending witnesses, the said G S having been first examined on oath by me as to the legality of such marriage; from which examination I became satisfied that there was no legal impediment thereto.

(*If the man is under twenty-one or the woman under eighteen years of age, and shall not have had a former husband or wife, and shall have a parent or guardian in the state, say*)

And I further certify that consent in person (*or in writing, as the case may be*) of T D, the parent (*or guardian*) of G S, he being under age, was duly given to me previous to such marriage.

Given under my hand at (*Milwaukee*), Wisconsin, on the —— day of ——, 18—.

J K,
Rector (*or Pastor*) of —— Church.

[*Indorse.*] My credentials of ordination were filed in the office of the Clerk of the Circuit Court for —— county, Wisconsin.

Sec. 10. If any person authorized by law to join persons in marriage shall knowingly solemnize any marriage contrary to the provisions of this chapter, or shall willfully make any false certificate of any marriage or pretended marriage, he shall forfeit for every such offense a sum not exceeding five hundred dollars, or may be imprisoned not exceeding one year.

Sec. 11. If any person shall undertake to join others in marriage, knowing that he is not lawfully authorized so to do, or knowing of any legal impediment to the proposed marriage, he shall be deemed guilty of a misdemeanor, and upon conviction thereof shall be punished by imprisonment in the county jail not more than one year, or by a fine not less than fifty nor more than five hundred dollars, or by both such fine and imprisonment, in the discretion of the court.

Sec. 12. No marriage solemnized before any person professing to be a judge, justice of the peace or minister of the gospel, shall be deemed or adjudged to be void, nor shall the validity thereof be in any way affected on account of any want of jurisdiction or authority in such supposed judge, justice or minister, provided the marriage be consummated with a full belief on the part of the persons so married, or either of them, that they have been lawfully joined in marriage.

Sec. 13. All marriages solemnized among the people called Friends or Quakers in the form heretofore practiced and in use in their meetings shall be good and valid, and shall not be construed as affected by any of the foregoing provisions in this chapter.

Sec. 14. It shall be the duty of every clergyman, justice of the peace, clerk, and of any other person or society, by or before whom any marriage may hereafter be solemnized or contracted, to make at once a record of the same in a book to be kept for the purpose, and within thirty days after such marriage to return the same in the form of a certificate, duly signed by the person so certifying, to the register of the county in which such marriage shall have been solemnized or contracted, which said record or certificate shall set forth, as far as the same can be ascertained, the full name of the husband, his occupation, and the name of his place of birth and residence, the full name of the wife previous to the said marriage, the names of the parents of said husband, and of the parents of said wife, also the color of the parties, and the time, place where and ceremony by which such marriage was contracted, and if pronounced by any clergyman or other person as aforesaid, the place of residence of such person; and if any person whose duty it shall be to return such certificate shall neglect to return the same as provided by this section, he shall forfeit for every such neglect a sum not exceeding one hundred dollars nor less than twenty-five dollars: *Provided*, that such action shall not lie unless the same be brought before such certificate of marriage be actually delivered to the register of the proper county.

NOTE.—MARRIAGE CERTIFICATE TO FILE WITH REGISTER.

STATE OF WISCONSIN, }
—— COUNTY, } ss.

I hereby certify that on the —— day of ——, A.D. 18—, Mr. —— —— and Miss —— —— were with their mutual consent legally joined together in holy matrimony by me in the presence of —— ——, and —— —— of ——, having been first satisfied by the examination of the said —— —— on oath duly administered by me, that there was no legal impediment to such marriage. And I ascertained the following facts as required by law, to wit:

1. Full name of husband.
2. Full name of father of husband.
3. Full name of mother of husband.
4. Occupation.
5. Residence.
6. Birthplace.
7. Full name of wife previous to marriage.
8. Full name of father of said wife.
9. Full name of mother of said wife.
10. Time when marriage was consummated.
11. The town, county and state where marriage was consummated.
12. Color.
13. By what ceremony consummated.
14. Place of residence of person performing ceremony.

Given under my hand at ——, this —— day of ——, A.D. 18—.

J K,

Rector (*or Pastor*) of —— Church.

[*Indorse.*] Credentials recorded in —— county, Wisconsin.

Sec. 15. Any clergyman, justice of the peace, physician or other person, who shall neglect to comply with the provisions of section fourteen of this chapter, shall forfeit for such neglect a sum not less than fifty nor more than one hundred dollars.

CHAPTER XXI.

WISCONSIN STATUTES OF RELIGIOUS ASSEMBLIES.

Section 1. No person shall keep open his shop, warehouse or workhouse, or shall do any manner of labor, or business, or work, except only works of necessity and charity, or be present at any dancing, or any public diversion, show or entertainment, or take part in any sport, game or play on the Lord's day, commonly called Sunday; and every person offending shall be punished by a fine not exceeding two dollars for each offense.

Sec. 2. Every person who shall at any time willfully interrupt or molest any assembly of people met for the worship of God, or any member thereof, or any persons when meeting or met together for the performance of any duties enjoined on or appertaining to them as members of any religious society, or any wedding party or other company or assembly of peaceable citizens, or for the recitation or performance of or instruction in vocal music within the place of such meeting or out of it, shall be punished by fine not exceeding twenty dollars nor less than five dollars.

Sec. 3. For the purpose of the provisions of this chapter, the Lord's day shall be understood to include the time between the midnight preceding and the midnight following the said day.

Sec. 4. No person who conscientiously believes that the seventh or any other day of the week ought to be observed as the Sabbath, and who actually refrains from secular business and labor on that day, shall be liable to the penalties of the first section of this chapter for performing secular business or labor on the Lord's day or the first day of the week, unless he willfully disturb some other person.

Sec. 5. That any person who shall sell any intoxicating drinks, or any other articles of traffic, within two miles of any camp meeting or other religious assembly, without the written permit of the person or persons having the oversight and management of such camp meeting or religious assembly, or who shall otherwise willfully interrupt or disturb such meeting or assembly, shall be punished by a fine of not more than fifty dollars nor less than five dollars: *Provided*, that nothing herein contained shall be construed to prohibit any such sale at any regularly established store, tavern or other place of business, which may have been licensed or established previously to such meeting, and not with the intent to evade the provisions of this act.

Sec. 6. Any person who shall violate the provisions of this act, and who shall be notified by any person having charge of such meeting or assembly, or by any other person, that he, she or they are violating the law, and who shall, after such notice, continue in such violation, he, she or they shall forfeit and pay for every such offense a fine not less than five dollars nor more than fifty dollars, to be collected as hereinafter provided and paid over to the county treasurer, where the same as other fines are required to be paid for the use of schools.

Sec. 7. Any sheriff, coroner, justice of the peace or constable of the proper county, shall, upon view or information, and without warrant, arrest any person offending against this act, and shall seize any article of traffic or other property found in the possession of the person or persons so offending, and convey the same to a place of safety, and take the person or persons so offending before any justice of the peace, and shall make an inventory of the property so seized; and the said justice of the peace, upon complaint upon oath or affirmation of the officer apprehending such offender, or the oath of any other person, shall proceed forthwith to inquire into the truth of the accusation, and, if found true, such justice shall inforce the penalty prescribed by this act.

CONSTITUTION OF WISCONSIN.

ARTICLE I.

Sec. 8. The right of every man to worship Almighty God according to the dictates of his own conscience shall never be infringed, nor shall any man be compelled to attend, erect or support any place of worship, or to maintain any ministry against his consent; nor shall any control of or interference with the rights of conscience be permitted, or any preference be given by law to any religious establishments or mode of worship; nor shall any money be drawn from the treasury for the benefit of religious societies or religious or theological seminaries.

Sec. 9. No religious test shall ever be required as a qualification for any office of public trust under the state, and no person shall be rendered incompetent to give evidence in any court of law or equity in consequence of his opinions on the subject of religion.

CHAPTER XXII.

WISCONSIN STATUTES OF RELIGIOUS SOCIETIES.

Section 1. It shall be lawful for all persons of full age, belonging to any church congregation or religious society, not already incorporated, to assemble at the church or meeting house, or other place where they statedly attend for divine worship, and by a majority of votes elect any number of discreet persons of the church congregation or religious society, not less than three nor more than nine in number, as trustees (a majority of whom shall in all cases be actual communicants of such church congregation or religious society), to take charge of the estate and property belonging thereto, and to transact all affairs relative to the temporalities thereof.

Sec. 2. It shall be lawful for any such church congregation or religious society to choose their minister to be the president of the said corporation and of their meetings by a vote as aforesaid; and at the election provided for in this chapter every person of full age who has statedly worshiped with such church congregation or society, and has been formally considered as belonging thereto, shall be entitled to a vote.

Sec. 3. The minister of such congregation or society, or in case of his death or absence, one of the elders or deacons, church-wardens or vestrymen thereof, and for the want of such officers, any other person being a member or stated hearer in such church congregation or society, shall publicly notify the congregation of the time when and the place where the said election shall be held at least fifteen days before the day of election; and such notification shall be given for two successive Sabbaths on which such church congregation or society shall statedly meet for public worship preceding the election.

Sec. 4. Any two of the elders, deacons, church-wardens or vestrymen of such church congregation or society, or if such officers shall not be present, then any two voters present, to be nominated by a majority of the voters, shall preside at such election, receive the votes, and determine the qualifications of voters; and they shall, immediately after the election, certify under their hands and seals the names of the persons elected to serve as trustees, in which certificate the name by which the said trustees and their successors in office shall forever thereafter be called and known, shall be particularly mentioned and specified.

FORM OF CERTIFICATE.

The undersigned, two of the elders (*or deacons, or church-wardens, or vestrymen, or voters*) of the (*church congregation or society*) hereafter mentioned, do hereby certify that on the —— day of ——, 18—, a number of persons, of full age, belonging to the church (*or congre-*

gation) of ——, a religious society assembled at ——, where they statedly attend for divine worship, in the town of ——, county of ——, and State of Wisconsin, for the purpose of organizing as a corporation, did, by a majority of votes, elect A B, C D and E F (*not less than three nor more than nine*), discreet persons of said church (*or congregation, or society*) as trustees, a majority of whom are communicants of said church (*or congregation, or society*), to take charge of the estate and property belonging thereto, and to transact all the affairs relative to the temporalities thereof. And it was then and there determined, by a like majority of votes, that the said trustees and their successors in office shall forever thereafter be called and known by the name and title of (*here give the name in full of the religious society*).

Witness our hands and seals this —— day of ——, 18—.

O P. [SEAL]
R S. [SEAL]

Sec. 5. Such certificate shall be acknowledged by the persons making the same, or proved by a subscribing witness thereto before some officer authorized to take the acknowledgment of deeds, and recorded, together with the certificate of such acknowledgment or proof, by the register of deeds of the county within which the church or place of worship of such congregation shall be situated, in a book to be provided by him for that purpose, who shall be entitled to receive seventy-five cents for such recording; and thereafter

such trustees and their successors shall be a body corporate by the name expressed in such certificate.

NOTE.—For form of acknowledgment see *ante*, page 125.

Sec. 6. The several clerks of the board of supervisors in this state not yet supplied with suitable books for recording the certificates aforesaid, shall immediately procure such books at the expense of the respective counties.

Sec. 7. Such trustees may have a common seal and may alter the same at pleasure, and they may take into their possession and custody all the temporalities of such church congregation or society, whether the same shall consist of real or personal estate, and whether the same may have been given, granted or devised, directly or indirectly, to such church congregation or society, or to any other person or persons for their use.

Sec. 8. Such trustees may also in their corporate name sue and be sued in all courts and places, and they may recover and hold all the debts, demands, rights and privileges, all churches, buildings, burial-places, and all the estate and appurtenances belonging to such church congregation or society, in whatsoever manner the same may have been acquired, or in whose hands soever the same may be held, as fully and amply as if the right and title thereto had been originally vested in the said trustees; and they may hold other real or personal estate, and demise, lease and improve the same, but the whole of such estate, real and personal, shall not exceed the yearly value or income of three thousand dollars.

Sec. 9. The said trustees shall also have authority to alter and repair their church and meeting houses, and under the direction of the society or congregation to erect churches and meeting houses and dwelling houses for their ministers, and other buildings for the use of their church congregation or society.

Sec. 10. They shall also have authority to make rules and orders for managing the temporal affairs of such church congregation or society, and to dispose of all moneys belonging thereto, and to order and regulate the renting of pews or slips in their churches and meeting houses, and the perquisites for the breaking of the ground in the cemetery or churchyard and in the said churches and meeting houses for burying the dead.

Sec. 11. They may appoint a clerk and treasurer of their board, and a collector to collect and receive their rents and revenues, and may regulate the fees to be allowed to such clerk, treasurer and collector, and may remove them and appoint others in their stead at pleasure; and such clerk shall enter all rules and orders made by such trustees, and payments ordered by them, in a book to be procured by them for that purpose.

Sec. 12. Any two of the trustees may at any time call a meeting of the trustees, and a majority of them being lawfully convened shall be competent to do and perform all matters and things which such trustees are authorized to do and perform.

Sec. 13. The said trustees shall hold their offices for three years, and until their successors are elected; and immediately after their first election, as hereinbefore provided, the said trustees shall be divided by lot into three classes, numbering one, two and three; and the seats of the first shall be vacated at the end of the first year, of the second class at the end of the second year, and the seats of the third class at the end of the third year, to the end that as near as may be one-third part of the whole number of trustees may be annually chosen.

Sec. 14. It shall be the duty of the clerk of said trustees, at least one month before the expiration of the office of any of the said trustees, to notify the same in writing to the minister, or in case of his death or absence, to the elders or church-wardens, and if there be no elders or church-wardens, then the deacons or vestrymen of any such church congregation or society, specifying in such notice the names of the trustees whose office will expire; and the minister or other officers receiving such notice shall, in manner aforesaid, notify the members of such church congregation or society of such vacancies, and appoint the time and place for the election to supply the same: *Provided*, if the clerk shall fail for any cause to give the notice as hereinbefore required, or the election shall not be held at the time as hereinbefore required, the church congregation or society shall not, for that reason, be dissolved or in the least affected thereby, but the notice and election may be held on some other day.

Sec. 15. All subsequent elections shall be held and conducted by the same persons and in the same manner as hereinbefore provided for the first election; and in case any vacancy shall happen by the death of a trustee, his neglect or refusal to act with the board of trustees for the space of two months or more, or removal from said society before his term of office expires or otherwise, notice thereof shall be given as aforesaid, and an election shall be held and another trustee chosen in his stead for the remainder of such term.

Sec. 16. No person belonging to any such church congregation or society incorporated under the provisions of this chapter, shall be entitled to vote at any election after the first until he shall have been an attendant on public worship in such church congregation or society at least six months before such election, and shall have contributed to the support of such church congregation or society according to the usages and customs thereof.

Sec. 17. The clerk of trustees shall keep a register of the names of all such persons as shall desire to become stated hearers in the said church congregation or society, and shall therein note the time when such request was made; and the said clerk shall attend all subsequent elections in order to test the qualifications of such voters in case they shall be questioned.

Sec. 18. Nothing in this chapter contained shall be construed to give to such trustees the power to fix or ascertain the salary or compensation to be paid to any minister, but the same shall be ascertained and fixed by a majority of such society entitled to vote at the election of trustees.

Sec. 19. It shall be lawful for the circuit court for the county in which any such religious corporation shall have been constituted, or in vacation for the judge of the judicial circuit in which said county is situated, on the application of such corporation, if such court or said judge in vacation shall deem it proper, to make an order for the sale or mortgage of any real estate belonging to such corporation, and to direct the application of the moneys arising therefrom to such uses as the said corporation, with the approbation of said court, or in vacation of said judge, shall conceive to be for the interest of such corporation. And when such order shall be granted by said judge in vacation, it shall be filed with the clerk of said court and entered of record in the same manner as if it had been granted by the court.

Sec. 20. At least ten days' previous notice of any such application to the circuit court, or in vacation to the judge of said judicial circuit, shall be given by publishing the same in some newspaper published in the county, if one be published therein, and if not, by posting up notices in three or more public places in such county.

Sec. 21. The provisions of sections nineteen and twenty of this chapter shall be applicable to all religious societies and corporations in this state, whether constituted under the provisions of this chapter or otherwise.

Sec. 22. Every church congregation or religious society heretofore incorporated in pursuance of law, and not since dissolved, shall be and is hereby established and confirmed, and in case of the dissolution of any such corporation, or of any corporation hereafter to be formed in pursuance of the provisions of this chapter for any cause whatever, the same may be incorporated under the provisions of this chapter at any time within six years after such dissolution; and thereupon all the estate, real and personal, formerly belonging to the same and not lawfully disposed of, shall vest in such corporation as if there had been no such dissolution.

Sec. 23. All lands, tenements and hereditaments that have been or may hereafter be lawfully conveyed by demise, gift, grant, purchase or otherwise to any persons as trustees, in trust for the use of any religious society organized or which may hereafter be organized within this state, either for a meeting house, burying-ground, or for the residence of a preacher, shall descend, with the improvements, in perpetual succession to and shall be held by such trustees in trust for such society.

Sec. 24. Whenever by the constitution, rules or usages of any particular church or religious denomination, trustees are required to be appointed by any minister, presiding elder or other officer or officers of such church or denomination, it shall be the duty of such minister, presiding elder or other officer or officers, to give to such trustees a certificate of their appointment, under the hand and seal of the person making the same, specifying the name by which such trustees and their successors shall forever thereafter be called and known, which certificate shall be acknowledged or proved and recorded as hereinbefore directed; whereupon such trustees and their successors appointed in the same manner shall be a body corporate by the name expressed in such certificate, with all the rights, powers and privileges of other religious corporations constituted according to the provisions of this chapter.

Sec. 25. Whenever by the constitution, rules and usages of any particular church or religious denomination, the minister or ministers, elders and deacons, or other officers elected by any church or congregation, according to the constitution, rules or usages, are thereby constituted the trustees of such church or congregation, it shall be lawful for such minister or ministers, elders and deacons, or other officers, to assemble together and execute under their hands and seals a certificate, stating therein the name by which they and their successors in office shall forever thereafter be called and known, which certificate shall be acknowledged or proved and recorded as hereinbefore directed; whereupon such persons and their successors in office shall be a body corporate by the name expressed in such certificate, with all the rights, powers and privileges of other religious corporations constituted according to the provisions of this chapter.

Sec. 26. Every church, parsonage and schoolhouse belonging to any religious society, with the land belonging thereto, not to exceed in all three acres in any one town, village or township, or, if in a city, not to exceed one lot for each of the said buildings, shall not be subject to taxation for any purpose except for its own improvement.

Sec. 27. Personal property owned by any religious, scientific, literary or benevolent association, used exclusively for the purposes of such association, and the real property necessary for the location and convenience of the buildings of such associations, and embracing the same, not exceeding ten acres, if not leased or otherwise not used for pecuniary profits, and including parsonages, whether of local churches or districts, and whether occupied by the pastor permanently or rented for his benefit, and in case of a chartered college or university: *Provided*, the lands are reserved for grounds of the institution not exceeding forty acres. The occasional leasing of such buildings for schools, public lectures or concerts, or the leasing of the parsonage as aforesaid, shall not render them or either of them liable to taxation.

Sec. 28. It shall be lawful for any Protestant Episcopal church incorporated within the state, by its trustees, officers or agents, now holding or who may hereafter hold the temporalities thereof, to convey them for or without a valuable consideration to the trustees of the funds and property of the Episcopal church, however called, acting within this state, to be held, sold or conveyed according to the direction of the diocesan convention or council of the Episcopal church in the state: *Provided*, that such conveyance shall not be made except upon notice and order of the court or judge as required in case of sale of real estate.

Sec. 29. The rector, wardens and vestrymen being the trustees of each Protestant Episcopal church incorporated in this state, may be chosen at such times and in such manner as may be in conformity to the rules and usages of such church, and elections or appointments of such officers heretofore made in conformity to such rules and usages are declared to be valid.

Sec. 30. Each Protestant Episcopal church heretofore or hereafter incorporated within this state, may take by purchase, devise, gift or otherwise, and may forever hold any lands intended to be used for cemetery grounds or burial purposes; and all grants, gifts, conveyances or devises of land heretofore made to any incorporated Protestant Episcopal church shall be valid and effectual, according to the intent of the parties.

Sec. 31. Sections fourteen, fifteen, sixteen of chapter sixty-seven of the Revised Statutes, shall apply to all lands so heretofore or hereafter acquired or held for burial purposes.

Sec. 32. All bonds and files relating to any corporation, now in the office of the clerks of the several boards of supervisors of this state, shall by said clerks be immediately transmitted to the office of the register of deeds of the proper county, to be by said register preserved in a convenient form for the inspection of any and all persons interested.

Sec. 33. Any five or more male persons of lawful age, not members of any religious congregation, desirous of forming a society for the promotion of the Christian religion in connection with a church to be associated therewith, according to their own peculiar tenets, may become incorporated, possess, have, hold and enjoy, all the rights, privileges and franchises incident to such corporations, as hereinafter provided.

Sec. 34. Such persons shall execute under their

hands and seals a certificate substantially in the following form:

Know all men by these presents, That we (*insert the names*), whose names are hereunto subscribed, have agreed and by these presents do agree to become incorporated into a religious society in pursuance of the laws of this state by the name and style of the (*here insert the corporate name*) of the (*here insert the name of city, village or town*); and we do hereby agree that all persons who may hereafter become associated with us in this organization shall be entitled to equal privileges and rights in the grants and franchises hereby secured under and by virtue of the statutes in such cases made and provided.

In witness whereof we have hereunto set our hands and seals this —— day of ——, 18—.

Sec. 35. The certificate thus executed shall be acknowledged before some person authorized to take acknowledgments of deeds, and shall be recorded in the office of the secretary of state, and copies thereof duly certified by him shall be received as evidence of the fact of incorporation, and for all other proper and lawful purposes, in all courts of law and equity. The secretary of state shall be entitled to receive fifty cents for recording each certificate, and the like sum for each certified copy thereof.

NOTE.—See form for acknowledgment, *ante*, page 125.

Sec. 36. That upon the recording of such certificate in the office of the secretary of state, the persons named therein shall be deemed and regarded in law as corporators, and they and their associates are hereby declared to be a body corporate and politic with perpetual succession by the name and style designated in such certificate, and by such name and style shall be competent to contract and be contracted with, to sue and be sued, to answer and be answered unto, in all courts of law and equity; and shall also be competent in law to purchase, have, hold and enjoy property, both real and personal, and to sell, dispose of and convey the same: *Provided, however*, that it shall not be lawful for such corporation to deal in property of any kind, except so far as shall be necessary for the legitimate objects of the corporation as declared in this act; *and provided further*, that the real estate to be held shall not exceed five lots in any city or village, or forty acres in the country not platted into lots.

Sec. 37. That every such corporation thus created may have a common seal, and alter and renew the same at pleasure, and may also adopt a constitution and by-laws for their government not inconsistent with the laws of this state or the United States, and may alter and amend the same at pleasure; and may also designate the number and title of their officers, and may also define their power and duties.

Sec. 38. A majority of the corporators named in such certificate may meet at such time and place as to them shall seem fit and proper for the purpose of perfecting their organization under the corporation thus secured; and the said corporators shall constitute the first board of trustees of the society, and shall hold their offices until others are chosen.

Sec. 39. Every society in this state composed of

persons who have united themselves together for the purpose of maintaining, as a body corporate, public worship or other religious exercises, which for the term of five years has maintained an actual organization by the election of officers, maintenance of public worship, or such other acts as are usual in conducting the operations of incorporated religious societies in this state, shall be deemed to have been legally incorporated, and shall have all the rights and powers and shall be subject to all the liabilities of religious societies duly incorporated under the laws of this state; but any society desirous of obtaining the benefit of this act shall be permitted to do so only upon filing in the office of the register of deeds in the county in which said society is situated a certificate, executed by three officers of said society, in the following form:

STATE OF WISCONSIN, }
COUNTY OF ——, } ss

A B, C D and E F, of the county of ——, do hereby certify that they and each of them are trustees (*or other officers*) of the ——, a religious society located at ——, in said county; that during five years immediately preceding the date hereof the said society has maintained an actual organization by the support of public worship with ordinary regularity (*or in other manner, stating how*), and that such organization has been maintained with the intent to maintain a corporate existence under the laws of this state.

Dated ——.

A B,
C D,
E F,

Sec. 40. Such certificate shall be verified by the officers making the same before some person authorized to administer oaths, and shall be recorded at length by the register of deeds of said county in the book in which the certificates of the organization of religious societies are recorded, upon the payment of his fees therefor; such certificate when so recorded, or the said record, or any duly certified copy of such record, shall be received as evidence in all courts in this state, and shall be *prima-facie* proof of the facts in said certificate set forth.

NOTE.—The foregoing chapter upon religious societies is embraced in chapter LXVI, Taylor's Statutes, except Secs. 27 28, 39 and 40.

Since these statutes were published there have been several acts passed, probably with the intention of making the law more complete, but which have had a tendency to confuse the whole subject; and as the statutes of the state are now under revision, and the law on this subject will likely be condensed and brought into a harmonious whole, they are not embodied in this work. They are as follows:

Chapter CXXIII, Laws of 1875: Providing that any diocesan council or convention, synod or other representatives of any church, may elect trustees, and by filing a certificate in the office of the secretary of state, stating the name of the body and of the trustees so elected, may receive a patent constituting them a corporation.

Chapter CCCCXI, Laws of 1876: Providing tor the incorporation of any Christian or Hebrew church which has been or may be organized in any town, village or city. This law seems to annul certain portions of the statute relating to religious societies, and it is doubtful what force and effect it has in that respect.

INDEX.

COMMON LAW OF MARRIAGE.

Affinity of parties 16–19–20
Age of parties to marriage 12–13
Absence for five years of one, other to marry 22
Archbishop Parker's table of prohibited degrees 20–21
Blind persons may contract marriage 15
Chancellor Walworth's opinion 10
Chancellor Kent's opinion 10
Cohabitation after marriage 10–15
Consent of party 10
of parents or guardian 13
Contract of marriage 7–8–9–13
Church of England's service 16
Consanguinity and affinity 16–19–20
Colored races, marriage with 21
Canon law, what it is 27
Common law, what it is 27
Civil law, what it is 28
Deaf mutes may contract marriage 15
Deceased wife's sister, not to marry 18–20
Daughter of deceased wife, not to marry 20–21
Disabilities to contract marriage 13
Divorced husband or wife, when may marry 22
Divorced for adultery, second marriage void 23
Force or fraud avoids contract 13–14
Form of marriage ceremony 26–27
Husband and wife 8
Husband's son, may not marry 20
Impediments to marriage 12–22
Impotency of party 15
Inability for copulation 15
Incestuous marriages 18
Imprisonment for life annuls marriage 22
Idiots and lunatics not capable to contract 13

Intoxication 13
Kindred, marriage with 19-21
Law, canon, common and civil 27-28
Levitical degrees 16-17
law 18-20
Marriage, the foundation of social order 7
in Protestant countries 7
when performed by clergy 7
indissoluble 8
who may contract 8
cannot be dissolved by parties 8
what constitutes 9
a civil contract 9
no particular form of requisite 10
in the United States 11
among Quakers 11-12
religious form of 11
who may contract 12
of consent 12-13
with wife's daughter 20
between whites and negroes 21
without ceremony 23-25
form of solemnization of 25
form of ceremony of 26-27
Malformation an impediment 15
Ministers of Protestant Episcopal church 23
Mormons, marriage among 11
Mutual agreement to marry 10
Protestant Episcopal church, canon of 23
Quakers, marriages of 11-12
Relation by affinity 19
Roman Catholic doctrine of marriage 12
law, what 28
Sentence of imprisonment for life annuls marriage 22
Sister of deceased wife, marriage of 18
Son of deceased husband, marriage of 20
Void and voidable contracts 15
White and colored races, marriages of 21
Wife's daughter, not to marry 20
Wife's relations 19

STATUTES OF ILLINOIS.

Age of parties to be joined in marriage 29
Burying-grounds, how laid out 40
Congregations may be reincorporated 40

Constitutional provisions as to religion...................... 34
Clergymen admitted to visit prisoners 35
Corporations, religious societies to be......................... 37
how organized.. 37-41
not dissolved by failure to elect trustees..................... 38
Disturbing religious assemblies, penalty for.................. 35-36
Incestuous marriages 29
Intention of marriage to be published......................... 30
Insane persons and idiots not to marry......................... 29
Legitimate and illegitimate children.......................... 29
License to be granted to parties to marry 29-30
Marriage, by whom celebrated................................. 29
how celebrated 29
license, form of 30
certificate of... 31
ceremony of.. 26-27
with certain kindred, incestuous............................... 29
Ministers to celebrate marriage............................... 29
Meetings, religious, penalty for disturbing 36
Peddlers not allowed at camp-meetings......................... 36
Penalty for neglect of duty by county clerk.................... 32
for neglect of duty by ministers................................ 32
Property of church exempt from taxation...................... 41
Public funds not to be applied to religious societies 34
Religious societies, incorporation of 37
may hold real and personal estate........... 39-40
trustees of, term of office.................................... 38
may mortgage or sell real estate 40
Real estate for camp-meetings not to exceed forty acres........ 41
for church purposes not to exceed ten acres.................... 39
Religion and religious assemblies............................. 34
Religious freedom protected.................................. 34
Sunday-school tracts may be distributed. 41
State's attorney to prosecute actions for penalty 33
Trustees of religious societies, how removed 39
Taxation, property exempt from.............................. 41
Word, trustees to include wardens and vestrymen 41

STATUTES OF INDIANA.

Age of parties to contract marriage.............................. 42-43
Assemblies, religious, penalty for disturbing.................. 58-59
Certificate of marriage, form of 44
of election of wardens and vestrymen to be filed............. 47
of election of wardens and vestrymen, form of................ 47-48
Churches dissolved may be revived, how....................... 51

may form union, how ... 51
shall file certificate of union, form of ... 52
Clergymen not to disclose confidential communications ... 59
Constitutional provisions ... 60
Consent of parent or guardian to marry, when necessary ... 43
Corporations, religious, to hold real and personal property ... 49-56
Election of trustees for religious societies ... 54
Friends or Quakers not required to procure marriage license ... 42
License to authorize marriage, when necessary ... 42-43
Marriage, a civil contract, how solemnized ... 42
when void ... 42
between whites and negroes, void ... 42
one party insane or idiotic, void ... 42
when not void ... 42
certificate of, to be filed ... 43
ceremony, form of ... 26-27
Ministers, duties on solemnization of marriage ... 43-44
exempt from toll on plank roads ... 60
Money, public, not to be applied to religious uses ... 61
Name of church or congregation, how changed ... 49
Organization of religious societies ... 54
Penalty for disturbing religious meetings ... 58-59
for performing marriage contrary to law ... 44-45
for violating Sunday law ... 59
Religious societies, how incorporated ... 54
freedom guaranteed ... 60
Sunday, labor and sporting prohibited on ... 59
Seventh day kept as Sunday ... 59
Taxation, property exempt from ... 60
Toll on bridges, parsons exempt from ... 60
Trustees appointed by united church ... 51
Wardens and vestrymen, how elected ... 46
and vestrymen, powers and duties ... 49
and vestrymen, vacancy filled ... 49
and vestrymen may take and hold real estate ... 49

STATUTES OF IOWA.

Assemblies, religious, penalty for disturbing ... 72
Clerk of circuit court, duty of ... 62-65
Certificate of marriage ... 63-64
Corporations, organization of ... 66-71
academical ... 69
to receive and hold property ... 70
how name changed ... 70
not dissolved by failure to elect trustees ... 69

Denominations having peculiar mode of entering marriage... 65
Husband responsible for return of marriage to clerk 65
Illegitimate children, how become legitimate................. 65
License to marry, when required................................ 62
Marriage a civil contract.. 62
ages of persons to contract.................................... 62
when a nullity.. 62
license necessary, when 62
by whom solemnized.. 63
certificate, form of.. 64
consent to, of parents or guardians........................... 62-63
registry of.. 65
of minors.. 63
ceremony of... 26-27
Ministers, not allowed to disclose confidential communications 74
their duties in solemnizing marriages......................... 63-64
Misdemeanor, to solemnize marriage contrary to law....... .. 63
to disturb religious assemblies............ 72
Penalty for failing to return marriage to clerk................. 64
for disturbing religious assemblies............................ 72
for solemnizing marriage contrary to law....................... 65
Priest not allowed to disclose confidential communications. ... 74
Religious societies, incorporation of.......................... 66
name of to be stated... 66
certificate of association 66-67
trustees, how elected.. 68
not to have same name as another............................. 69
Sabbath, labor on, prohibited.................................. 73
penalty for violation of..................................... 73
Seventh day, when kept as Sabbath 73-74
Spirituous liquors not to be sold near religious meeting....... 72
Testimony may be taken before license to marry granted...... 63

STATUTES OF MICHIGAN.

Acts relating to religious societies.............................. 95
Age of parties to contract marriage......................... 75
Assemblies, religious, penalty for disturbing............... .. 96
Bishop or other officer not to have corporate power............ 92
Certificate of marriage, form of............................... 81
Churches may sell or mortgage real estate 87
may make application to court 91
heretofore incorporated, how reëstablished.................... 94
dissolved, how reincorporated................................ 94
customs and canons of, not to affect real estate................ 93
Constitutional provisions relating to religion................ 97-98

Examination of party to marriage, form of 77
Exempt, property of religious societies, what 98
Idiots and lunatics not allowed to marry 76
Marriage, a civil contract 75
age of parties to contract 75
degrees within which prohibited 75
impediments to 75
of whites and negroes prohibited 76
by whom solemnized 76
oath of party to 77
witnesses to 78
ceremony, form of 26-27
certificate, form of 81
record, form of 80
Misdemeanor to join persons in marriage without authority .. 78
Money not to be appropriated to religious denominations 98
Oath of parties to marriage, form of 77
Penalty for joining persons in marriage contrary to law 78
for neglect to file certificate of marriage 82
Quakers, marriage of 79
Record of marriages to be made by minister 79, 80
Religious societies, incorporation of 83
articles of association of 83
certificate of election of officers 85-86
Trustees, powers of 87
to sell and convey real estate 87
to make application to court 91
Taxation of church property 98
Witness necessary to marriage 78

STATUTES OF MINNESOTA.

Acknowledgment to certificate of incorporation, form of 125
Certificate of marriage, form of 103
Church, Prot. Episcopal, election of wardens and vestrymen 120-121
Constitutional provisions as to religious freedom 109
Corporations heretofore dissolved may organize anew 114
Illegitimate children legitimatized by marriage of parents 106
Labor, gaming, etc., prohibited on Lord's day 107-108
Lord's day, what time to include 109
Marriage, a civil contract 99
consent of parties to, essential 99
age of parties to contract 99
impediments to 99
by whom solemnized 99
one of the parties to, to be examined on oath 100

form of oath of parties to........ 100
form of examination and note........ 101
license to parties to, how issued........ 101
ceremony, form of........ 26-27
certificate of........ 103
Meetings, religious, protection of........ 107-108
Ministers to file credentials of ordination........ 100
Penalty for performing marriage contrary to law........ 104
for failure to deliver certificate to clerk........ 104
for disturbing religious assemblies........ 107-108
Protestant Episcopal Church, to elect wardens and vestrymen 120-121
Quakers, marriage among........ 105
Religious assemblies, disturbing........ 107
corporations, how organized........ 110
corporations, trustees of, how elected........ 110-115
corporations, notice of election of trustees of........ 110
corporations, certificate of election of trustees of........ 111
corporations, trustees of, powers and duties of........ 113
Record of marriage, how made........ 103-104
of election of trustees of corporations........ 112
Societies, religious, existing, confirmed........ 117
Spirituous liquors, sale of, prohibited at camp-meeting........ 107
Trustees of religious societies, powers and duties of........ 113
term of office........ 114
election of........ 111-113
Witnesses to marriage ceremony........ 102-103

STATUTES OF OHIO.

Age of persons to be joined in marriage........ 126
Board of trustees, of religious societies........ 140
how perpetuate succession........ 140
of united societies........ 145
vacated, how filled........ 140-152
Ceremony of marriage, how regarded........ 131
form of........ 26-27
Clergymen, duties of........ 135
to keep registry of deaths........ 135-136
to keep registry of marriages........ 136
to make report of marriages........ 136
neglecting to report marriages, penalty for........ 136
neglecting to report deaths........ 136
not to testify to confessions........ 136
Consent of parents or guardians, when required........ 128
form of........ 130
Constitutional provisions as to religion........ 135

English language, religious services to be conducted in......... 143
Fine or forfeiture, how recovered................................ 131
for selling liquor near religious meetings...................... 133
Interrupting religious meetings, penalty for................. 132
Land to descend to trustees of religious societies................ 141
License to ministers to marry.................................. 126
to parties to marry, when necessary........................... 127
Marriage, parties to and age of................................ 126
license to be granted to parties................................ 127-128
who may solemnize.. 126
bans, how published... 127
consent to, of parents or guardians............................ 126-128
party to, to make oath... 128
certificate of, transmitted to probate judge.................... 128
form of certificate of.. 129
ceremony, form of 26-27
between whites and negroes forbidden 131
Misdemeanor for interrupting religious meetings............ 132
Ministers of the gospel to solemnize marriage................ 126
license to solemnize marriage................................ 127
credentials of ordination..................................... 127
Notice of election of trustees for religious societies............ 150
Penalty for marrying persons contrary to law 129
for marrying persons, not being authorized 129
for marrying whites with colored persons...................... 131
for interrupting religious meetings............................ 132
Petition to sell real estate of religious society.................. 142-148
Presbyterian societies, how to elect deacons.................. 154
Publishing houses established by religious societies........... 154
Probate judge to grant licenses................................ 127
to take oath of witness 128
Process, how served upon religious societies 147-149
Real estate of religious societies, how conveyed 141-142-147
Record of proceedings of religious societies.................... 150
of marriage, how made... 128
of credentials of ministers..................................... 127
of marriage, when evidence.................................... 127
Religious assemblies, interrupting of....... 132
persons to be expelled from................................... 132
Religious societies, how incorporated 137
election of trustees 137
record of proceedings... 139
name of 150
to convey real estate... 141-146
to be corporations.. 148
neglect to elect trustees, not dissolved.......................... 152

Repeal of law not to affect vested rights........................ 149
Seventh day observed as Sunday, when........... 135
Succession of property of religious societies.................. 150
Sunday, violations of.................. 134
Trustees of religious societies, how elected. 150
term of office.. 137–150
acceptance of office....... 139
certificate of election 139–150
to be not less than three...................................... 137
form of certificate of election... 138
their powers and duties....................................... 138–150
to hold property.. 148
failure to elect.. 152
Trust property of religious societies, how held.................. 141
Union of two or more religious societies.......................... 143
ratification of.. 144
certificate of, to be filed..................................... 145
White and colored persons forbidden to marry.................. 131

STATUTES OF WISCONSIN.

Acts relating to religious societies................................ 182
Camp-meetings, law protecting 164
Certificate of marriage to be returned.......................... 161
of marriage, form of, to be filed 161
of election of trustees, form of 168–169
Churches heretofore incorporated reëstablished 174
Church parsonage not subject to tax........................... 176
extent of land.. 176
Circuit court may order sale of lands of corporations........... 173–174
Constitutional provision as to religious freedom 165–166
Corporations, religious societies to be....................... 170
Election of trustees of churches, how conducted............... 168
Exemption of church property from taxation.................. 176
Friends or Quakers, marriages among 160
Intoxicating drink prohibited near meeting 164
Lands held by trustees to descend to trustees................... 175
Lord's day, what time to include.............................. 164
Marriage, a civil contract...................................... 155
consent of parties to 155
consent of parents or guardians to............................ 157
age of parties to contract..................................... 155
impediments to... 155
by whom solemnized.. 155
examination of one of parties to 156
oath of one of parties to...................................... 156

form of examination of parties to 157
form of consent of parent to 158
two witnesses required to 159
ceremony, form of 26–27
certificate to give to parties to 159
certificate to give to parties, form of 159
not void for want of authority 160
record of, to be made 160–161
Ministers, to file credentials 156
to notify congregations of elections 168
appointing trustees to give them certificate 168–175
Money not to be drawn from treasury for religious uses 166
Male persons of full age, how incorporated as society 178
to file certificate 178
powers and duties as such 180
Penalty for performing marriage contrary to law 159–160
for performing marriage, not being authorized 160
for not returning record of marriage 161–162
for disturbing religious meetings 163
for labor on Sunday 163
Protestant Episcopal Church, may convey property 177
wardens and vestrymen, how chosen 177
to hold cemetery lands 178
Record of marriages to be made 161
Religious assemblies, penalty for disturbing 163
spirituous liquors, sale prohibited at 164
Religious societies, how incorporated 167
to elect trustees 167
qualification of voters 167–173
trustees of, powers and duties 170
may sell real estate 170
Religious tests not required 166
Society maintaining public worship, to be body corporate 181
to file certificate 181
Sunday, labor and gaming prohibited on 163
what time to include 164
Seventh day observed as the Sabbath 164
Traffic in liquors and other articles prohibited at meetings 164
Trustees of religious societies, term of office 171

www.ingramcontent.com/pod-product-compliance
Lightning Source LLC
LaVergne TN
LVHW011222110826
845150LV00006B/1507

* 9 7 8 1 4 2 5 5 1 5 5 2 2 *